W9-BLZ-377

# More Praise for *The Principal*

"This revealing and powerful book comes just in time, as we launch the biggest education reform in the past fifty years. It should be required reading not only for principals, but perhaps even more importantly for those who support and lead them."
—**Laura Schwalm**, CaEdPartners; former superintendent, Garden Grove, California

"After decades of studying, working with, and enhancing the lot of principals . . . Fullan's conclusion? Principals are needed now more than ever, and he's smack on target. He doesn't mince words, yet instills hope and confidence. Simply great . . . this book should be on every leader's desk. Another bullseye!"
—**Willam Parrett**, director, Center for School Improvement and Policy Studies, Boise State University, Idaho

"I am on fire and in love with this book. Fullan's uniquely succinct brilliance for soaring above the noise and clutter that bogs us down is, as always, energizing and inspiring. *The Principal* stirs my mind and my heart."
—**Alice Thomas**, president and chief executive officer, Center for Development and Learning, Metairie, Louisiana

# THE PRINCIPAL

## Three Keys to Maximizing Impact

*Michael Fullan*

Cover image: Walter B. McKenzie, Getty (RF)
Cover design: John Hamilton Design

Copyright © 2014 by John Wiley & Sons, Inc. All rights reserved.

Published by Jossey-Bass
A Wiley Brand
One Montgomery Street, Suite 1200, San Francisco, CA 94104-4594—www.josseybass.com

No part of this publication may be reproduced, stored in a retrieval system, or transmitted in any form or by any means, electronic, mechanical, photocopying, recording, scanning, or otherwise, except as permitted under Section 107 or 108 of the 1976 United States Copyright Act, without either the prior written permission of the publisher, or authorization through payment of the appropriate per-copy fee to the Copyright Clearance Center, Inc., 222 Rosewood Drive, Danvers, MA 01923, 978-750-8400, fax 978-646-8600, or on the Web at www.copyright.com. Requests to the publisher for permission should be addressed to the Permissions Department, John Wiley & Sons, Inc., 111 River Street, Hoboken, NJ 07030, 201-748-6011, fax 201-748-6008, or online at www.wiley.com/go/permissions.

Limit of Liability/Disclaimer of Warranty: While the publisher and author have used their best efforts in preparing this book, they make no representations or warranties with respect to the accuracy or completeness of the contents of this book and specifically disclaim any implied warranties of merchantability or fitness for a particular purpose. No warranty may be created or extended by sales representatives or written sales materials. The advice and strategies contained herein may not be suitable for your situation. You should consult with a professional where appropriate. Neither the publisher nor author shall be liable for any loss of profit or any other commercial damages, including but not limited to special, incidental, consequential, or other damages. Readers should be aware that Internet Web sites offered as citations and/or sources for further information may have changed or disappeared between the time this was written and when it is read.

Jossey-Bass books and products are available through most bookstores. To contact Jossey-Bass directly call our Customer Care Department within the U.S. at 800-956-7739, outside the U.S. at 317-572-3986, or fax 317-572-4002.

Wiley publishes in a variety of print and electronic formats and by print-on-demand. Some material included with standard print versions of this book may not be included in e-books or in print-on-demand. If this book refers to media such as a CD or DVD that is not included in the version you purchased, you may download this material at http://booksupport.wiley.com. For more information about Wiley products, visit www.wiley.com.

*Library of Congress Cataloging-in-Publication Data*

Fullan, Michael.
  The principal : three keys to maximizing impact / Michael Fullan. --First edition.
    pages cm.
  Includes bibliographical references and index.

ISBN 978-1-118-57523-9 (cloth)
ISBN 978-1-118-58245-9 (ebk.)
ISBN 978-1-118-58254-1 (ebk.)

1. School principals. 2. Educational leadership. 3. Educational change. 4. Educational innovations. 5. School management and organization. I. Title.
  LB2813.9.F85 2014
  371.2—dc23

                          2013043206

Printed in the United States of America

FIRST EDITION
*HB Printing* 10 9 8 7 6 5 4 3

# ALSO BY MICHAEL FULLAN

# CONTENTS

# PREFACE

IN 1988, I DEALT MYSELF SOME SERIOUS MARCHING ORDERS IN A monograph titled *What's Worth Fighting for in the Principalship?* And the long march goes on. In several recent books that I'll cite later in this text, I've continued that work by trying to define the new kind of change leadership that principals need to embody, especially now as formalized standards of achievement and ever-evolving technology increasingly influence how schools are to be run. What I haven't done until now is to explore and discuss in detail how (and why so urgently) the principal's role now needs to change.

So in this book we come to grips with the oft-cited idea that the principal is the second most important factor (next to the teacher) in influencing student learning. It turns out that the impact of the principal lies neither in micromanaging instruction nor in autonomous entrepreneurialism. Even the new roles for principals as direct instructional leaders that are emerging this decade will and should become rapidly outmoded.

This book is somewhat U.S.-centric partly because the key issues are so clearly in contrast in that country, and partly because the United States is big and complex and so consequential if the improvement of schooling is not addressed effectively.

But the issues I take up are relevant to any country in the world. In any case, in the chapters that follow, I will show how the principal's role in any public school system should change, and provide enough evidence to indicate that it can be done, and on a very wide scale in short order. The messages and the direction are clear, and are aimed at incumbent and aspirant principals and all those who work to make schools more powerful learning systems.

The bottom line is that life could change markedly for the better for the principal. I will show what the new role of the principal can be, why it is exciting, and how principals can maximize the impact they have on students and teachers. If you are a school leader, this is why you came into the profession and assumed a leadership role. If you are a district or system leader, this is what you dream of—scores and scores of principals doing great things for the system as a whole. There is no time to waste!

⸙   ⸙   ⸙

To download discussion questions and a Professional Development Training Kit, visit www.wiley.com/go/theprincipal. The password is the last five digits of this book's ISBN, which are 27239.

# ACKNOWLEDGMENTS

I RECEIVED FEEDBACK FROM SEVERAL PEOPLE WHO KNOW the principalship deeply, representing collectively a couple of hundred years of experience being inside and close to the role. Although any shortcomings that remain are mine, I deeply thank them for all their insights: James Bond, Lucy Calkins, Rick DuFour, John Hattie, Lyle Kirtman, Ken Leithwood, Kathy Reidlinger, and Alice Thomas. I am especially indebted to my core team of Claudia Cuttress, Eleanor Adam, and Joanne Quinn, and to the recent expanded team of Maria Langworthy and Santiago Rincon-Gallardo, who produce so much and of such high quality. And to Andy Hargreaves, always a great team player.

Thanks to my many other partners in learning over the years: Steve Anderson, Sir Michael Barber, Alan Boyle, Miguel Brechner, Kathy Budge, Greg Butler, Carol Campbell, Carmel Crevola, Katelyn Donnelly, Mary Jean Gallagher, Peter Hill, Bill Hogarth, Lisa Kinnman, Tony MacKay, John Malloy, Eleanor Newman, Bill Parrett, Charles Pascal, Roger Quarles, Clif St Germain, Laura Schwalm, Sir Ken Robinson, Geoff Scott, Peter Senge, Lyn Sharratt, Lew Smith, and Nancy Watson.

Special thanks to the principals and staff of three schools I filmed in May 2013: Andreas Meyer, William G. Davis Sr. Public

School, and Lawrence De Maeyer, Central Peel Secondary School, both in Peel District School Board (in the northwest part of the greater Toronto area), and James Bond of Park Manor in Elmira, Ontario, of Waterloo Region District School Board (west of Toronto); and to Tony Pontes, director of education of Peel, and his senior staff. We learned a lot about the new roles of the principals, staff, and students through this filming.

Thanks also to the scores of policymakers, teachers, and administrators with whom we have teamed up to make improvements in action through which we all are learning so much. These partners in whole-system improvement include tens of thousands of leaders in Ontario at the school, district, and government levels; all the superintendents in Alberta; a large and ever-growing number of Californians, including those in schools and districts, the CTA (the teachers' union), Governor Jerry Brown, the state superintendent, Tom Torlakson, and Christy Pichel, Davis Campbell and the Stuart Foundation, who supports our work in that state; and leaders across Idaho, every part of Australia, and all four Nordic countries. There is also a burst of new energy in Latin America, including Chile, Mexico, Peru, Uruguay, and other South American countries rapidly on the move.

My appreciation goes to the team at Jossey-Bass—Lesley Iura, Marjorie McAneny, and Alan Venable—great developmental editors (a euphemistic term for the people who tell authors that given chapters are more clutter than clarity) who improved the manuscript immensely. And a tribute to the Ontario Principals' Council (OPC), in particular Ian McFarlane and Joanne Robinson, who have advocated broad global views of the principal's role; OPC has copublished nearly all of my books.

After living through and always supporting my writing over the years, the members of my immediate family—Wendy, Bailey, Conor—seemingly take the next book in its stride, but they can't fool me; I recognize and appreciate their ubiquitous support.

All in all, lucky me.

# ABOUT THE AUTHOR

**Michael Fullan, Order of Canada**, is professor emeritus at the Ontario Institute for Studies in Education, University of Toronto. He served as special adviser in education to Ontario Premier Dalton McGuinty from 2003 to 2013 and has been awarded honorary doctorates from the University of Edinburgh, University of Leicester, Nipissing University, Duquesne University, and The Hong Kong Institute of Education. Fullan consults with education systems around the world, focusing on whole-system change. He is the award-winning author of more than thirty books, including *The Six Secrets of Change*, *Stratosphere*, *Professional Capital* (with Andy Hargreaves), *Motion Leadership in Action*, and *Change Leader*. To learn more, visit www.michaelfullan.ca.

ONTARIO
PRINCIPALS'
COUNCIL

Exemplary Leadership in Public Education

# Mission

To promote and develop exemplary leadership for student success in Ontario's schools

# Purpose

The purpose of the Ontario Principals' Council is to

- Represent its membership
- Promote the professional interests of its members
- Support and protect its members
- Advocate on behalf of public education
- Provide professional growth opportunities for principals and vice principals

# Logo

There are three major components to the Ontario Principals' Council: the provincial structure, local OPC groups, and individual members. The logo represents the intersection of these components where all parts of OPC work together in support of the organization.

# CHAPTER · ONE

# Outmoded

The learning fates of principals, teachers, and students are intimately interrelated—and in the past decade, the conditions for mutual learning in schools have been seriously eroding. Students are bored, to put it mildly. Two-thirds of initially happy kindergartners become alienated from schooling by the time they reach grade 9 (Jenkins, 2013). Teacher satisfaction has declined 24 percent since 2008, when 62 percent of them reported feeling "very satisfied"; within five years, only 38 percent were saying that (Metropolitan Life Insurance Company, 2013). Meanwhile and not unrelated, 75 percent of principals feel that their job has become too complex, half of all principals feel under great stress "several days a week," and the percentage who say they are satisfied in their work has dropped from 68 to 59 since 2008. In other words, students, teachers, and principals are keeping pace with each other, but unfortunately *in the wrong direction*.

Ask teachers what school they would most like to teach in, or whether they want to stay in teaching at all, and you will hear of two criteria that top their lists: the quality of their colleagues and the quality of school leadership. Insofar as principals choose or seem to choose their teaching staff, the principal alone is often held responsible by districts and others for the collective plummeting of morale. Even among themselves, 90 percent of principals think that they are the ultimately accountable person (Metropolitan Life Insurance Company, 2013). If you happen to be a principal yourself, you most likely feel a huge burden of accountability. But as we shall see, many of the current solutions to the problems I've noted here not only don't help—they make matters worse.

# Gasp!

Principals' responsibilities have increased enormously over the past two decades. They are expected to run a smooth school; manage health, safety, and the building; innovate without upsetting anyone; connect with students and teachers; be responsive to parents and the community; answer to their districts; and above all, deliver results. More and more, they are being led to be direct instructional leaders, and therein lies the rub. How is this for a shocker: the principal as *direct* instructional leader is not the solution! If principals are to maximize their impact on learning, we must reconceptualize their role so that it clearly, practically, and convincingly becomes a force for improving the whole school and the results it brings. I will show that the latest conceptualizations of the principal's role inhibit the influence that principals could have over instructional improvement in the school, and for that matter in the district and beyond.

The heart of this book is to reposition the role of the principal as overall instructional leader so that it maximizes the learning of all teachers and in turn of all students. In the meantime, the role has become more and more problematic. The current concept of what principals should do is either confusing (What exactly does instructional leadership mean anyway?), too narrow (What is being neglected as we become preoccupied by classroom instruction?), too tedious (checklists, checklists, checklists), or impossible (How do I reach all those teachers, or how can I be an expert in every subject?).

The new Common Core State Standards (CCSS) curriculum will make these tensions unbearable because so much more will be expected of schools and their principals. We have put the principal on a pedestal, and now we expect miracles; a few can pull it off, but mere mortals have little chance. Under these conditions, the idea of principal as instructional leader cannot survive on any significant scale. There is an alternative that I will lay out in the coming chapters. This repositioning of the principal will yield learning results that are wider and deeper, and eminently more doable in the bargain. The future for the principal can be exciting and profoundly significant for school and system improvement. By re-centering the role of the principal, we bring the ideal of principal as key change agent within our grasp.

New, rapidly emerging change dynamics almost organically favor a different and more powerful role for principals, and really for all—students, teachers, parents, administrators, and policymakers. Tensions are growing between, on the one hand, an urge to tighten the focus around standards and, on the other hand, a tendency to allow digital innovations to flourish. The capacity to navigate, indeed to help others navigate these troubled waters will require a new kind of leadership. We will see that this new view of leadership has the advantage of being more in harmony with the human condition. Humans are fundamentally motivated by two factors: doing things that are intrinsically meaningful to themselves, and working with others—peers, for example—in accomplishing worthwhile goals never before reached. If principals can get the knack of stimulating and enabling these organic forces, then fundamental changes will occur in rapidly accelerating time frames, transforming stodgy or moribund school systems into dynamic learning environments. This is not an abstract, theoretical statement. All of my work is based on "practice producing better theory," rather than the reverse. Put another way, in my work with schools and districts, I am already seeing new theories of change in action that motivate students, teachers, and administrators to do things collectively that they find more engaging and more productive for learning.

Consider an analogy to epidemiology. Health scientists try to detect and understand the sources of rapidly spreading diseases. Such diseases have a life of their own. The goal of the scientists is to figure out how to stop disease from spreading. This is often very hard to do, but possible. But let's flip the issue. What if the phenomenon's spreading were a good thing contributing to better health and well-being? It would still be hard to stop, but the leader's job would be different than the epidemiologist's. The leader would have the exciting role of facilitating the spread of the disease, so to speak. To ensure rapid spread, the leader would recognize and uses forces within the "germ" itself. The leader would thus become a curator of positive contagion. Enough fancy talk. Let's get down to the realities of what this would mean in practice.

# Leading Learning

In this book, we will sort out the details of what is problematic about the current role of the principal and how it can shift to that of an agent of contagion and fundamental change. In another recent work, I called this type of role "motion leadership," meaning the kind of leadership that causes positive movement forward (Fullan, 2013b).

Until now, no one has sufficiently clarified the new role of the principal and given principals the detailed attention required in order to enable schools to thrive under the new conditions. Aspects of the new role of the principal have been around for a while in the work of those of us focusing on collaborative cultures, learning communities, and capacity building (DuFour & Marzano, 2009; DuFour & Fullan, 2013; Fullan, 2010a; Leithwood & Seashore Louis, 2012). Hargreaves and I (2012) went further with our concept of "professional capital of teachers." Further offshoots of a deeper role for school leaders are occurring as my colleagues and I foster the *new pedagogy* (defined as students and teachers working together as learning partners) merging with the *digital world* (Fullan, 2013b; Fullan & Donnelly, 2013; Fullan & Langworthy, 2014). Ironically, these developments, old and new, are being undercut by recent, intensified, wrongheaded conceptions of the principal as instructional leader. We will get to this, but first let's frame the new role of the principal as I see it emerging.

I have been using the word "role," but what I really have in mind is a trio of parts, the most central of which is *learning leader—one who models learning, but also shapes the conditions for all to learn on a continuous basis.* The term "learning leader" isn't new, but for our purpose, I will endeavor to make it precise, memorable, and "sticky"—a draw for clear action. Call it also "leading learner" or "lead learner" if you like. Flanking that part of the role, at this stage of our redirection, will be two others: *system player* and *agent of change.*

## Maximizing Impact

So this book focuses on what principals should do if they want to lead learning in ways that clear the path toward improving student achievement in demonstrable ways. In it, I will make no claims for the role of leading learning that cannot be linked to *measurable impact, deep and wide.*

My colleague Ken Leithwood coined a statement you've likely heard more than once by now: "The principal is second only to the teacher in terms of impact on student learning" (Leithwood, Seashore Louis, Anderson, & Wahlstrom, 2004, p. 5). But if the principal is that crucial, and I for one concede this point, the questions it begs are surely *what* impact can principals have, and *how* can they maximize that impact? As answers, lots of proposals crop up in the massive literature on the principalship, but there is also a great deal of noise. My goal is to make simple but powerful sense of the role of the principal in leading learning. The idea is that if you are a principal or aspiring to become one, after reading this book you will know what to focus on in order to make the biggest difference. And those of you who are system leaders will know how to best take advantage of, leverage, and support lead learners like yourself.

In the same way that we can become mere tenders of floods of information, principals can fall to the mercy of myriad expectations. So in this book, let's boil the task down to the smallest number of big levers and liberate the system by liberating the principal—not as a free agent, but as an ensconced player who makes good things happen. If the principal really is the second most important factor in student learning, let's see how we can enable him or her to function as such—with maximum results.

## This Watershed Moment

A quarter of a century ago, I published *What's Worth Fighting For in the Principalship?* (Fullan, 1988). It turns out that 1988 was a watershed year for principals. Although it wasn't entirely clear at the time, 1988 was almost literally the beginning of what we might call the "instructional" period; that is, it was in this period that schools began to shift from a focus on the individual autonomy of the classroom and the isolation of the school toward a focus on specific instructional practices that directly affected student learning and achievement. The very first large-scale districtwide instructional initiatives occurred in the 1988–1996 period in District 2 in New York City with Tony Alvarado, and in Toronto with our Learning Consortium. Several of us began to focus systematically on instruction across all schools in the district, with the principals as key players. The role of the principal shifted dramatically toward an instructional focus, but it was also the case that the system was throwing the principal off kilter with enormous demands. *What's Worth Fighting For* focused on what you as a leader could do to empower yourself and those around you to take action that made a difference in the lives of students under your watch. I cited a survey from Ontario in 1984 that asked principals what were the most significant new responsibilities that had been added to their roles in recent years. The two most frequently named additions as of 1984 were teacher performance review, and curriculum implementation! Déjà pre-vu! In any case, the role changed, and principals have been working their way through the new role as instructional leader for the past twenty-five years.

Today we are at another watershed moment. The recommended detail-specific instructional role of the principal (what I call micromanaging) is turning out to be ineffective for creating change at any significant scale. The flip side of this current narrowness—the knee-jerk reaction perhaps—has been to afford the principal greater autonomy in exchange for high-stakes accountability: "polish or perish!" This book attempts to cancel that dysfunctional tug-of-war and locate a substantially more powerful lead learner role for principals that, as you will see, centers on fostering what Hargreaves and I call the professional capital of teachers in highly specific ways. I present not a broad solution but a precise one. It will require great leadership skills, but ones that can be learned by any good educator.

I will also try to take into account two major changes of circumstance represented by the Common Core State Standards (CCSS) and continuing digital innovation. With these, the stakes and demands have become greater. CCSS is blanketing most of the United States with a very complex set of demands, and technology is running wild. Both of these phenomena represent great opportunities within themselves, but they are also very challenging and in many ways have unclear implications for implementation. Once again, in this book we look to school principals to play a leading role, positioning them as central players. This opportunity to recast the role of the principal should not be missed. Although it is true that a prime quality of today's principal will be the ability to handle ambiguity, I can guarantee that the new role will be engaging, achievable, and ultimately more clear and more fulfilling. Best of all, it is learnable and brings with it the deep satisfaction of maximizing learning for scores of students who are not now being served by the school system. The principal as lead change agent could become one of the most prized educational roles around.

# The Chapters That Follow

Chapter Two reflects on how, frustratingly, the greater the sense of urgency, the greater the anxiety and the worse the attempted solution. It also examines how and why we keep "getting it wrong," and ends on a promising note that new virtues are around the corner if we focus on them and take action.

Chapter Three seeks to capture the essence of the new "leading learning" role as it plays out within the school, guided by the concept of building the school's *professional capital*. We will see what this asset looks like and how it's amassed, and indicate why developing teachers' professional capital, individually and collectively, is an increasingly powerful alternative. Chapter Four shows why it is crucial—for one's own school and for the district—that principals become district players, valuing peers as much as themselves and keeping an eye out for the system as a whole. Again I make the case that this is both doable and effective. In Chapter Five, we zero in on the principal as change agent in order to identify the core competencies of the new leadership. These elements of the change agent in action, or "motion leadership"—the kind of leadership that moves individuals, organizations, and systems forward—have the virtues of being succinct in number, practical to implement, and efficient in the sense that any one element serves two or more skill sets.

Chapter Six—"The Future Is Now"—provides an exciting ending, showing how the principal's role is likely to change for the better because it is part of a system dynamic. Because the current system is boring for students, alienating for teachers, and frustratingly unproductive for policymakers and the public (these elements constituting what I call the "push factor"), and because the new pedagogy, the digital world, and the change dynamics of positive contagion (the "pull factor") are unstoppable, it is a dead certainty that new opportunities will present themselves in numbers. The chapter takes the increasing presence of new technologies of the digital world as one new challenging theme and the CCSS as another. Both will require skilled principals who can think independently as well as act as part of the team and the system.

## Still Worth a Struggle

The period we are entering will not be simple. There are many ways to go wrong. I can only guarantee that it will be dynamic and that the qualities of lead learners will be the order of the day.

This time around, what's worth fighting for is to lead learning and to maximize impact whereby *the system as a whole dramatically (and I do mean dramatically) improves.* The rest of the book will help you as a principal do this, and it will make clear how district and system leaders should work with school leaders to make this happen.

# Action Items

☐ Rate your work satisfaction right now compared with prior years. Ask your teachers how they rate their own.

☐ What signs (subtle or strong) do you see among your more advanced students of growing love or dislike of school?

☐ What percentage of your students do you think are heading toward dropping out in the future?

☐ As a principal, for what do you consider yourself accountable? Are you "in charge" in those respects?

☐ How much of your time now goes to direct instruction? Where else does it go?

☐ What roles do you play now as principal?

# Discuss with Colleagues

- Where are your schools headed right now, and what implications does this have for how teachers can work together more effectively?

- How effective has the principal's involvement in direct instruction been at changing the school as a whole?

- What watershed moments have you experienced as an educator?

# CHAPTER · TWO

# Vices and Virtues

This chapter is about a vicious circle in which principals in the United States increasingly find themselves trapped; the next will be about a more virtuous cycle that establishes and sustains the conditions for success. The principal needs to become a balanced leader—minimizing the counterproductive actions and specializing in the generative actions that yield positive results.

## Panic Time?

Do you feel a terrible sense of urgency? Or is what you feel these days more like panic? John Kotter (2008), a long-standing change leader guru, has a great take on the concept of urgency. He says, true enough, that big changes can't be initiated without some terrible sense of urgency, but once we leave the starting blocks, the need is to focus our efforts. Without focus, urgency makes things worse, becoming what Kotter calls "a false sense of frenetic urgency" rather than the "true sense of urgency" that forges and allies itself with forces of actual change. Which is it for you: the false urgency that accompanies persistent failure, including repeatedly failed solutions; anxiety, frustration, anger, and a feeling of "what a mess"; and frenetic activity to cure the problem, running from one unlikely remedy to another? Or an urgency that focuses a powerful desire to win, right now; a sense of great opportunities coupled with the realization that there are hazards everywhere; and relentless, fast-moving, alert activity directed toward important issues? Perhaps we should simplify that description to a focus that purges irrelevant activities in order to free up time and energy for ideas that hold real promise.

Urgency can push one off or on course, as this chapter will suggest. And once we get off course, our urgency pushes us further afield. A start that gets a critical matter wrong will make the situation worse. A start that gets it right will turn crisis into breakthrough. Which type of bike are you riding? The one whose spokes spin "virtuous circles," or the one that turns out to be "vicious"?

Although it is true that things can deteriorate faster than they can be mended, it doesn't take that much longer for the right dynamic of factors to create lasting, powerful solutions. When effective actions replace ineffective ones, they motivate people to do even more. As we will see later, substantial progress can kick in within a two-year period and become stronger after that, but only if you avoid what I have called the "wrong" policy drivers.

## Four Wrong Choices for Driving Policy

A principal is not always in all respects the person in the driver's seat, foot on the pedal, hands on the wheel. So some of what I plan to say here applies equally to others who would steer and pace the principal's daily ride at work.

I don't mean to question motives. When one is facing a crucial situation, it is easy to do the wrong (meaning the ineffective or counterproductive) thing, especially if one does not feel entirely in charge. But even when one is constrained by external conditions, there is always leeway for action. Here as elsewhere I will try to keep the main points few in number.

We can start with a brief portrayal of the big picture in the United States that has taken us to the current crisis and its accompaniment—panic that makes matters worse. The United States has been in a constant state of urgency for three decades, ever since the publication of *A Nation at Risk* (National Commission on Excellence in Education, 1983), with its famous rallying cries that the foundation of America's education system was being eroded "by a rising tide of mediocrity," and that if a foreign power were to try to impose the system of education that existed, we would have considered it as "an act of war." The time had come to declare a new "Imperative for Education Reform," as the subtitle of the report claimed. There was an urgent need to compete economically in an increasingly competitive global world, and education was to be the route. Quality for all was to be the answer. Unfortunately, there was no discernible strategy that derived from the report or its aftermath. A crisis without a strategy is a recipe for random action and growing frustration.

The next stab at reform was the ambitious No Child Left Behind (NCLB), a bipartisan education act passed in 2001 that President George H. W. Bush signed in January 2002. Representing cumulative frustration about the lack of progress, NCLB mandated that all students would be tested in grades 3 through 8 in reading and math, and that all students would be required to achieve "adequate yearly progress" (AYP) in their test scores. Individual schools that failed AYP for two years in a row would be subject to escalating consequences including eventual closure. Moreover, states would be required to have a "qualified teacher" in every school by 2006. Finally, every child was to obtain proficiency in the basic tests by 2014. There was no national framework—each state was required to have standards and tests, but was left to decide on the actual standards.

Now we had a discernible strategy: the wishful thinking of undefined standards with no particular way of enacting them. I hope you are beginning to appreciate how this ill-conceived world is beginning to close in on the principalship.

This brings us to the present, when in 2009 President Obama introduced the current education policy under the banner of Race to the Top. Acknowledging that NCLB was too prescriptive, the new legislation was based on four components: new standards and assessments; massively improved assessment and data systems; greater quality of teachers and principals via recruitment, appraisal, rewards, and punishment; and a focus on turning around the bottom 5 percent of schools. Finally, although this is not the place to elaborate, the CCSS also entered the scene, endorsed by over 90 percent of the states that have signed on to define world-class standards in English language arts and math and to develop corresponding assessments aligned to these new standards. The work on standards and assessments is well under way, with an assessment system to be established by 2014–2015.

What is the principal to make of all this? As well intentioned as the reforms might be, the fact is that the principal is being led to a role that narrows the sphere of influence he or she can have. To be explicit, "standards and accountability" are exceedingly weak strategies for driving reform. For a deeply insightful parallel analysis applied to the teaching profession, see Jal Mehta's book *The Allure of Order* (2013).

Mehta shows how the evolution of standards and accountability as applied to the teaching profession with greater intensity over the years has fundamentally weakened the effectiveness of the profession. His brilliant conclusion is that policymakers are trying to do at the back end with accountability what they should have done at the front end with capacity building. De-professionalization is the only outcome of such a strategy. I will show in this book how this predominance of "back-end accountability" is boxing in the principal in ways that will not end well for the principal or for the system as a whole.

In previous work, I have framed the problem in terms of the interplay of "wrong" and "right" policy drivers. In particular, four main, interrelated barriers, what I call the wrong drivers—each of them basically an error of perspective—keep the principalship stranded on the shoulder of the high road of school success.

By drivers, I mean policies and associated strategies—usually set by federal entities, states, or districts—that are intended, well, to "drive" a school or larger system to new levels of success. Wrong drivers do not always look obviously wrong, and they are not wrong topics to consider, but the evidence pertaining to the four I will discuss here, illustrated in Exhibit 2.1 (from my paper "Choosing the Wrong Drivers for Whole System Reform," 2011a), is that, as *drivers*, they do not actually produce the desired results. They get people off on the wrong foot. Adjacent to each wrong driver listed is a better alternative. Do keep in mind that right and wrong are nearly always questions of context, and the context here is defined by the need for *change*.

Exhibit 2.1 Wrong vs. Right Drivers

| Wrong | Right |
|---|---|
| Accountability | Capacity building |
| Individualistic solutions | Collaborative effort |
| Technology | Pedagogy |
| Fragmented strategies | Systemness |

The four "right drivers" must form the foundation and guiding principles of action and integrate the beneficial aspects of the wrong drivers into the service of change. The wrong drivers can be attractive up-front because they look like quick fixes, can be legislated, and can appeal superficially to the public. In the final analysis, the right drivers guide and integrate the four wrong ones so as to create maximum benefit.

## Accountability

Accountability assumes that the most important thing to do is to make sure that a person down below acts in line with directions or criteria passed down by someone higher up. As a rigid priority and attitude, accountability belongs at the top of the wrong-driver chart because it permeates the others below it. It is understandable (but wrong) to conclude that because the education system often lacks focus, we must tighten it with strong direct accountability. Human systems are not that straightforward. At best, carrots and sticks work only in the short term, and always become dysfunctional in the middle to long terms, as Daniel Pink (2009), the observer of business, work, and management, has so convincingly shown in his book *Drive*, an examination of motivation. Even if you loosen the strict requirements of accountability and give local schools more leeway (in exchange for which they have to deliver greater accountability), results will not be obtained on any scale because local capacity cannot be assumed.

In our work in whole-system change, my colleagues and I have shown time and again that if you give people skills (invest in capacity building), most of them will become more accountable. In Ontario, for example, we have accomplished widespread improvement in literacy and high school graduation across the entire public school system of forty-nine hundred schools and seventy-two districts. We have no overt accountability beyond high expectations, investing in capacity building, increasing transparency of results and practice, and maintaining a relentless focus on progress. Accountability in the end works because people become increasingly committed to results, to their peers, and to the system as a whole. To take one example, York Region District School Board, just north of Toronto, with 180 schools and huge diversity, steadily improved its results in literacy, numeracy, and high school graduation over the first decade of this century employing these very strategies (Fullan, 2010a). There are countless other examples of this phenomenon, including many districts in the United States (DuFour & Fullan, 2013).

Think of the following analogy: capacity building is to accountability what finance is to accounting. Finance is about how people organize and invest their assets; if you have only accounting, you are merely keeping careful records while you go out of business! In the same way, there is more to accountability than measuring results; you need also to develop people's capacity to achieve the results. Extreme pressure without capacity results in dysfunctional behavior.

Tighten the screws of accountability, and people will game the system, as was demonstrated in Atlanta. From 2001 to 2009, the Atlanta public school system steadily increased its test scores, advancing its leader, Beverly Hall, to the distinction of superintendent of the year in 2009. By 2011, she had been indicted by a grand jury along with thirty-four other educators (teachers, instructional coaches, and principals), charged with creating a culture of endemic cheating whereby educators were encouraged to achieve targets at any cost (fabricating answers, falsely reporting results, and so on) and were protected and rewarded for doing so. Investigators found pervasive cheating at all levels of the system, which stunned many in the public and the nation. Maybe stunning on such a scale, but predictable when accountability makes targets so crucial that people will do whatever they can get away with to survive (or thrive in this case, as results were tied to financial bonuses for the superintendent). Reward the high performers and punish the low with a distorted accountability system, and many will engage in self-interested and counterproductive actions. If you are a principal "leading" a school in such a system, the best you can do is to get better at a bad game—do what you can to please the higher-ups in order to protect your staff and yourself. What starts on a small scale becomes a systemic problem—a culture of cheating.

Wrongheaded accountability is like pushing a train by building up power in the caboose. It is far more effective to *pull* humans than to try to push them. This is why the better alternative to simply demanding accountability is to aim at building capacity from the beginning, with an explicit focus on results. Paradoxically, this produces greater accountability, as people in groups are more likely to hold themselves accountable, because transparency puts on the right kind of pressure for greater performance and makes it easier and more effective to identify the true laggards, who turn out (after capacity building) to be very small in number—much less than 5 percent.

In the next chapter, I will show what capacity building is, especially with respect to what I call the professional capital of teachers, and how the principal can lead its development, yielding better results and more accountable behavior. It turns out that you have to get at accountability indirectly by improving the performance of individuals and the group. In short, accountability is achieved through targeted capacity building rather than directly.

## Individualistic Solutions

The fallacy of individualistic solutions—let's get better teachers, better school leaders—is that individuals do not change cultures very easily. In addition, you have to use the power of the *group* to change the group. Instead of allowing principals to focus on the group, current policies bog down principals in piecemeal individualism. Here principals are in double jeopardy. At the same time that they are prodded or persuaded to attempt to develop their staffs one teacher at a time, principals themselves are often handled that way by their districts. Let's see how both of these "solutions" founder, starting with the teacher.

Historically, teaching has been a "lonely profession" in which teachers operate their own kingdoms behind the classroom door. Current policymakers have identified the problem correctly in this respect: most teachers don't get feedback on their teaching and thus don't improve. No feedback for teachers, ergo no improvement—absolutely correct. But the form of "feedback" educational bureaucracies often resort to is of the carrot-and-stick variety, which results in a no-win, perennial cat-and-mouse game between principal cats and teacher mice. I will show how teacher appraisal schemes must be reconsidered. The primary tool for improvement in any organization is not one-to-one appraisal but rather cultures that build in learning every day and that use appraisal to supplement and strengthen the learning (and indeed take action in relation to persistent low performers). If the appraisal system is perverse—that is, if it becomes artificial and is not linked to clear improvement—leaders will either have to play the game or otherwise engage in something that they know is inauthentic. Effective principals, those who want to get something done, will figure this out and learn to work with teachers in ways that do not waste time or are counterproductive. As wise cats, they will find it more productive to join the mice.

The effort led by the Bill & Melinda Gates Foundation to develop effective measures of teaching effectiveness gets the problem half right: teachers need good feedback and normally don't get it. Thus we have witnessed an explosion in the development of instruments and frameworks for "teacher appraisal." Reinforced by Race to the Top legislation that I earlier reviewed as Mehta's "back-end accountability," the new evaluation "tools" that have been developed are being applied to individual teachers and tied to merit pay and other crude incentives. The theory of action is this: everyone knows that teachers are the single most important education force relative to student learning, so we must assess their performance and output, reward the best, and punish the clunkers. Do this for, say, a decade, and you will end up with a greatly improved teaching profession. Teacher appraisal instruments or tools are thus (erroneously) seen as the way forward.

Well, a fool with a tool is still a fool. What the carrot-and-stick policy purveyors don't get is that people simply don't improve that way; a few perhaps, but never many. Countries that have a strong teaching profession and legions of great teachers—such as Singapore, Finland, or Canada—did not achieve that state by using the crude method of reward and punishment. Instead, they established a "developmental" approach to making teachers more effective: they developed leaders, such as principals who could help teachers work together in a focused way to use diagnostic student data linked to the improvement of instruction in order to get better results; they operate in transparent ways so that people can learn from one another; they monitor progress and intervene when necessary. In short, they create high-performance expectations and cultures.

With current reform efforts, U.S. principals are caught in the middle, where they can decide to waste their time in either of two ways: they can dutifully engage in the time-consuming, low-yield activity of conducting appraisals and processing a system that garners little by way of results (including, by the way, dutifully assessing poor performance, only to find that the system does not back them up and that they are alienated from their teachers), or they can collude with teachers and go through the motions; that is, they can conduct perfunctory appraisals because they know the system does not work to improve teaching. There is a better way, as we will see in Chapter Three, where I describe how to create conditions under which feedback is not only constructive but listened to and acted on.

Until we change the current system—and my point is that policymakers are making it worse by intensifying dysfunctional back-end accountability—we will continue to get results like those reported by Jenny Anderson (2013) in the *New York Times*. Anderson notes that in the most recent teacher evaluations in Florida, Tennessee, and Michigan, 97 percent,

98 percent, and 98 percent of teachers, respectively, were deemed effective or highly effective. When the system is not carefully constructed to lead to actual improvement, principals engage in superficial appraisals. Even when they aim at improvement, the individual efforts—one teacher at a time—rarely add up. The answer is not to make the evaluations more rigorous, unless you want more cat-and-mouse activity.

In Chapter Four, I will reposition teacher appraisal so that it can contribute to teacher development as part of a more integrated system of improvement. In essence, in dealing with their staffs, principals should shift from focusing on one-to-one work with each individual teacher to leading collaborative work that improves quality throughout the faculty.

Now to the second jeopardy: how principals themselves are handled, another face of what I call the "individualistic bias" of reform strategies. Typically, districts and larger systems attempt to solve fundamental problems by producing more and better "individual leaders." The weakness of this solution is subtle. The point is not to stop developing better individual would-be principals, but rather to stop counting on them to save the day. These personnel or human resource actions are necessary, but not the first, most crucial point. The primary issue is to change the culture of the school and the district so that learning is the work—that is, so that people are getting better at what they do because learning to be more effective is built in to the values and routines of the organization. As day-to-day learning becomes the prime activity, districts can reinforce it with better personnel practices that attract, cultivate, and retain great leaders, including principals. But great leaders, one by one, will never change the culture. A wrong culture will absorb well-meaning individuals faster than we can produce them. We need to stop depending on Band-Aid remedies, and instead focus on changing the culture itself. And here, principals have a key role, as we shall see in Chapter Three.

Even seemingly very good examples of district reform reflect the individualistic bias, and in fact show how subtle this bias can be. Meredith Honig, an educational leadership and policy specialist at the University of Washington, and her colleagues conducted a detailed study of how three school districts "fundamentally transformed their work and relationships with schools to support districtwide teaching and learning improvement" (2010, p. iii). As they say at the outset of their report, "a striking feature of all three central office transformation efforts was the focus on building the capacity of school principals to lead for instructional improvement within their schools" (p. v). This sounds as though it is on the right track, but there is a subtle and powerful difference between focusing on *individuals* and developing *groups* (along with individuals). Let's pursue this critical distinction.

Honig and her colleagues point to the role of districts as they differentiated supports for principals, modeled ways of thinking and acting, provided tools and their use, and served as brokers between principals and external resources.

As one instructional leader of principals put it:

> "I . . . spend time in [schools] helping the principals . . . focus their work . . . Working on the quality of teaching and learning . . . Looking at best practices. Giving them feedback. [If I don't] . . . it is not going to pay out in dividends in the student achievement. Because . . . we are creatures of habit first of all. So taking a principal who has not spent time in their

classrooms and getting them to shift their focus takes a lot of . . . intentional work. And then to be able to maintain that focus in a culture where people [e.g., teachers] are used to . . . keeping you in an office to deal with this one [student] all day— that's a whole other level of work . . . And then helping people [principals] to prioritize their time so that they do spend time on the core business in the areas that matter the most." (Honig, Copland, Rainey, Lorton, & Newton, 2010, p. 27)

One of the three districts had a checklist of twenty-six instructional practices that principals should look for. Let me be crystal clear: these practices do increase the principal's knowledge of instruction and are useful for the professional development of principals, but they can in no way serve to *change the culture of the school as a whole, let alone the culture of the district*. There is nothing in the Honig report that describes what principals do to affect *groups of teachers*. This is not the fault of the researchers. These districts, all geared up for instructional focus, were attempting to improve teaching through the individual efforts of principals and other instructional leaders. It would be gratuitous to add, but I will anyway, that one of the districts was Atlanta. Instructional focus can be deceptive. What looks like an intense devotion to it may in fact be ineffective or even counterproductive. Instructional focus, as I will show in Chapter Four, must be very finely honed if it is to affect all the teachers.

Similarly, Corcoran, Casserly, Price-Baugh, Walston, Hall, and Simon's (2013) study of six districts, *Rethinking Leadership: The Changing Role of Principal Supervisors*, compounds the problem by adding another layer of supervisors who focus on individualistic instructional leadership of their principals.

There is good professional development here *to a point*. But the point is not to have layered individualism, but rather to influence the culture of focused collaborative work. There are a lot of good things in what the six districts consider to be important: reviewing school data, observing classrooms and student work, understanding the pedagogical shift in reading and writing instruction, using student performance data to improve classroom instruction, conducting principal evaluations, and understanding the shift in mathematics expectations, instruction and standards (Corcoran et al., 2013, p. 30). By tightening the links from principal supervisors to principals to teachers you can get a blip in increased performance (compared to the previous "loosely coupled" system) but you quickly reach a ceiling effect. Here is Corcoran et al.'s conclusion: "unfortunately, there is no data showing a direct link between student attainment and any one principal supervisory model or approach" (p. 53). There is no *direct* link because deeper change comes through both direct and indirect effects of individuals and groups working in a coordinated fashion. We will see that this work is nonetheless explicit, powerful, and of lasting value.

My point in this section is that attempting to solve system problems with individualistic strategies is as typical as it is ineffective. Individual leader development is a necessary but not sufficient solution to the challenges of achieving system effectiveness. Another problematic case in point is Turnbull, Riley, Arcaira, Anderson, and MacFarlane's otherwise useful study (2013) of six districts as they develop "the principal pipeline." If you only had to develop human capital, the pipeline might be OK, but it is an unfortunate metaphor. You stuff them in at one end, shape them uniformly, and pull them out the other end, where there is only one spout. We need pools of talent rather than pipelines (thanks to Andy Hargreaves for this concept; personal communication, September 2013). We need to shape the role so that principals are helped to work with "groups" and to learn from other principals as a way of changing the culture of the organization.

## Technology

The third pair of wrong and right drivers—technology versus pedagogy—is fascinating in its history. By and large over the past decades, the investment in technology has been largely a matter of acquisition—buy, buy, buy—not a matter of figuring out how pedagogy (new forms of instruction) can use computers, personal devices, software, and the like to deepen and accelerate learning. Larry Cuban (2013) arrived at a similar conclusion when he examined the role of technology over the last forty years and found no evidence of positive impact on the "black box of classroom practice." Thus the principal's valuable time is eaten up by pursuing technology funding or by managing how these new "gifts" purchased by districts and states can be retrofitted.

I will have more to say about technology in Chapter Six. In other work that my colleagues and I are engaged in, we are concluding that radical breakthroughs are occurring in schools where new technologies are being combined with new pedagogies (learning partnerships between and among teachers and students), generating productive innovations (Fullan, 2013b; Fullan & Langworthy, 2014). This new future, which is already upon us, will demand new leadership from the principal to lead the group in integrating technology and pedagogy in the service of deep learning. Chapter Six contains some examples of this new work in action.

## Fragmented Policies

Like technology as a driver, this last one also offers endless ways to fill a principal's day. Ad hoc or fragmented strategies turn a principal's job into one of keeping too many batons or chainsaws in the air, endlessly juggling ill-shaped, ill-timed, and uncoordinated policies. Even if particular initiatives are not in conflict, the overload of disconnected pieces becomes impossible to manage. Sometimes policies are "aligned" on paper but never seem to cohere in the minds of principals and teachers. The result is that principals are expected to lead the implementation of policies that they do not comprehend and that indeed are incomprehensible as a set. The better driver, for which "systemness" seems like a good word to me, functions to coordinate strategies and align the efforts they require. We don't need a fancy analysis for systemness. It is essentially the extent to which individual members identify with each other and with the overall system. It is not alignment on paper that counts but rather coherence in the minds of implementers. We will return to this solution later, but the key notion is that sound strategies are ones that produce coherence or shared mind-sets in the day-to-day lives of teachers and principals.

## Drivers in Perspective

The four misguided drivers I have just described are wrong choices for front-end forces for reforming a system, be it a single school or a district of them. They will not and cannot work to lead system change. It is not so much that we need to discard them, but more that they need to be repositioned to play a supporting role for the right drivers. In short, if you place primary emphasis on capacity building, collaborative effort, pedagogy, and systemness, and integrate accountability, human resource policies, technology, and specific policies as part of the overall strategy, you will achieve greater success overall.

# Too Broad, Too Narrow: The Transformative Versus Instructional Leader

Stubborn problems set us oscillating back and forth, like an unconfident boxer who weaves from side to side, believing he lacks the punch to win the bout. Over the years, educators and their mentors have cycled through a "too broad" period of supposing that what has come to be known as "transformative leadership" must be the key, then back to a "too narrow" period in which principals are expected to be right in there giving specific feedback to as many individual teachers as they can. If you have been in education long enough, you can get hit by the same pendulum more than once!

If you've been a principal for a while, you remember when transformative leadership was all the rage. Leaders were to become generally attuned to the moral imperative of raising the bar and closing the gap as they inspired teachers and others to new levels of energy and commitment. The shared mission was meant to become a rallying point for teachers *somehow* to accomplish things never before achieved. It was all *very* broad indeed. Specificity and clarity never ensued.

In reality, the evidence shows that the transformative leadership concept and movement simply didn't work. Viviane Robinson of the University of Auckland is a leading international education researcher specializing in leadership and school improvement. Conducting an in-depth meta-analysis of twenty-two studies, she and her colleagues found that the impact of transformative leadership was a puny 0.11 in effect size on student achievement (Robinson, Lloyd, & Rowe, 2008). (An effect size is a statistical measure of the degree of relationship between two variables—an effect size below .40 is considered to be weak or insignificant). Basically they found that creating a general inspiring vision and instilling motivation in teachers to join the cause were not specific enough to produce actual results. One can readily surmise that creating broad, even inspiring messages does not help much with the actual mechanics of getting where you want to go.

Robinson saw more promise at the narrower end. She found that what she called "instructional leadership" (what I call leading learning) had a significant (but still not impressive) effect size of 0.42. This finding and those of others have indeed raised the expectation that principals should become "instructional leaders." But what does that really mean? I realize that it is heretical these days to conclude that principals can engage in "too much" instructional leadership or, even more disturbing, to suggest that principals can have too much "moral imperative" (defined as a deep and relentless commitment to raising the bar and closing the gap in learning for all students), but in my view, the shift to instructional leadership has led the principalship down an unproductively narrow path of being expected to micromanage or otherwise directly affect instruction, as we shall shortly see.

The narrow view raises two problems: first, in complex matters, you can't really micromanage to good effect; second it can be incredibly time consuming for principals, diverting them from doing other things that can shape learning more powerfully. Supervising individual teachers into better performance is simply impossible if you have a staff of, say, more than twenty teachers. Principals who find themselves in districts that require that they spend X amount of time, say, two days per week, observing in classrooms will be less effective overall because they can't influence very many teachers in any given time period; they can't be experts in all areas of instruction; and they will end up neglecting other aspects of their role that would make a bigger difference, such as developing the professional capital of teachers as a group, along with other key aspects of leadership essential for motivating people to work together with the leader and others. (See Chapter Three.)

A similar point has been made earlier in an article by Richard DuFour and Robert Marzano (2009). (DuFour advanced through a long, distinguished career as teacher, principal, and superintendent to his current role as education writer and consultant. Marzano is another leading researcher and consultant whose practical translations of current research and theory into classroom strategies are internationally known and widely practiced.) As they put it, "time devoted to building the capacity of teachers to work in teams is far better spent than time devoted to observing individual teachers" (DuFour & Marzano, 2009, p. 67). But somehow these observations have been overshadowed by the accountability juggernaut. I asked Lyle Kirtman, who has spent the last decade identifying the competencies of effective education leaders (more about his findings in later chapters), if he had encountered the problem of too narrow a focus on instructional leadership. Within a nanosecond he fired off two examples:

One principal in a wealthy community received a vote of no confidence from her faculty. Her focus was on instructional leadership and the use of data to improve results for all her students. Her superintendent interviewed ten faculty members and found that her communication skills, her empathy for faculty and students, a lack of support for teachers on parent complaints, and her relationship to her principal peers in the district were extremely poor. Her leadership style was more on content and data and not strong in dealing with people. She was very angry about the superintendent's viewpoint because she believed that her instructional skills were exceptional and that it was difficult teachers that were the problem.

Another principal in a suburban district was focused on instruction and data analysis for students. She was confrontational with teachers about how they needed to improve. There were constant complaints from teachers about her lack of overall leadership skills. The superintendent finally received a vote of no confidence from the faculty and removed her as principal. (Personal communication, March 2013)

You could say that these two principals were not very good leaders—that they lacked emotional intelligence or even good managerial qualities—and that is the point. A narrow focus on instructional leadership and student achievement can shut out other dimensions of leading learning. And, strange as it may seem, being "deeply passionate" can lead to blind spots if you become overbearing—a phenomenon that Kaplan and Kaiser (2013) discuss in their book *Fear Your Strengths* (more about this issue in Chapter Five).

In short, in the current climate, it is easy to go overboard on instructional leadership. Principals need to be specifically involved in instruction so that they are knowledgeable about its nature and importance, but if they try to run the show down to the last detail, it will have a very brief run on Broadway indeed.

# Principal Autonomy and Micromanaging: Other Roadside Attractions

Another false step that is appealing on the surface is to strip away the constraints of bureaucracy by giving the school principal more autonomy in exchange for delivered accountability. Thus principals can be given more discretion over hiring staff and more flexibility with respect to budget and resources. New York City used this model, as have certain states in Australia recently. In these cases, individual schools are granted greater autonomy, but are expected to deliver strong accountability through teacher appraisal and student test results. This deal with the devil has several problems. First, not many schools have the capacity in the first place, so they could hardly do better if left on their own. Second, those that are most advantaged often are the first to respond, creating an even greater gap between the haves and the have-nots. Third, it's not that good a deal anyway. It puts everyone constantly on guard and makes it impossible for isolated successes to play any part in promoting a larger, more lasting solution. Thus, individual autonomy of schools is no more of a solution than individual autonomy of teachers.

The devil loves to tempt individual principals to go their own way. Autonomy is almost always preferable to being in a bad relationship (for example, a stifling bureaucracy), but the truth is that a good relationship is better still, and this is where my argument is heading. In the rest of the book, I will make the case that connected learning, within and across schools and systems, is the only way for whole systems to improve and keep improving.

## Micro Madness

The main point of this chapter is that principals are being led down a narrow path of instructional leadership that will ultimately prove futile. They are being called on to micromanage, whereby they go after instruction in detail, teacher by teacher. DuFour and Mattos (2013), both former principals now engaged in research, comment on what Race to the Top precision has spawned in Tennessee, one of the first states to win the grant. The model that the state proposed (and was funded to carry out) "calls for 50 percent of a teacher's evaluation to be based on principal observations, 35 percent on student growth, and 15 percent on student achievement data" (p. 36). DuFour and Mattos summarize the new role:

> Principals or evaluators must observe new teachers six times each year and licensed teachers four times each year, considering one or more of four areas—instruction, professionalism, classroom environment, and planning. These four areas are further divided into 116 subcategories. Observations are to be preceded by a pre-conference, in which the principal and the teacher discuss the lesson, and followed by a post-conference, in which the principal shares his or her impressions of the teacher's performance. Principals must then input data on the observation using the state rubric for assessing teachers. Principals report that the process requires four to six hours for each observation. (2013, p. 36)

One can readily surmise that if you are a principal in such as system, under intense scrutiny to cover all your assignments, you will either burn out or learn to go through the procedures superficially. In either case, actual improvement is the casualty. If it is any consolation to the Tennessees of the world, it is easier to shift from such micromanaging to what I call developing the professional capital of one's teachers than it is to shift from excessive individualism (and get anywhere at all). With excessive individualism, or greater autonomy, one does not necessarily develop expertise, whereas micromanagers at least develop expertise in instruction that can be useful in the service of collaborative work.

A good example of the contrast between autonomy and focused collaboration can be found in David Kirp's revealing study (2013) of Union City, New Jersey. Union City is a poor, crowded, Latino community that for much of the last quarter of the last century was the poorest-performing district in the state. That changed in the last decade. By 2011, 89.4 percent of the Union City students graduated from high school—15 percent more than the national average. Among other things, the Union City district got the principalship right, finding that "just right" productive ground between micromanaging and excessive autonomy. Kirp comments on nearby Trenton, a city that embraced what he calls "the great leader theory" (excessive individualism, in my words) whereby "superstar" principals were hired and given autonomy in exchange for delivering results. The results didn't materialize. In Trenton from 1999 to 2008, the percentage of students passing grade 8 math tests rose from 18.2 percent to 21.9 percent. (By comparison, in Union City, the corresponding figures were 42 percent to 71 percent.)

Union City has been successful because it focuses on developing and employing the professional capital of its teachers, principals, and schools. Kirp (2013) refers to Les, a principal who does understand her job in this fashion:

> Aside from observing and evaluating the teachers, Les needs
> to help them improve. One strategy is to break through the

isolation of the classrooms, encouraging teachers to work together, jointly devise projects for their students, and talk about what's working well in their classrooms and what isn't. Such collaboration, the evidence shows, can make a substantial difference in the quality of instruction. (p. 54)

Very few districts or states seem to grasp the critical distinction between focused collaboration and detailed micromanaging. The road to perdition that I am describing is paved with good intentions. Take the recent document from New Jersey, Student Growth Objectives: Developing and Using Practical Measures of Student Learning (New Jersey Department of Education, 2013). There follows quite a good, rational discussion of specific and measurable objectives linked to standards, based on prior learning, measured between two points in time. Teachers are then required to develop student growth objectives (SGOs), have them approved by the principal (or the principal's designee) by November, with any changes completed and approved by February; finally the teacher's supervisor scores the SGO, with the rating being discussed at the annual summary conference.

What starts as a reasonable proposition—let's be clear, know the individual students, and provide instruction accordingly—turns into one big compliance nightmare for teachers and principals alike. A good idea becomes an odious task. There is only one thing worse than having to carry out an odious task, and that is having to supervise those carrying out such tasks. This type of well-intentioned compliance regimen is being replicated around the country in the name of accountability. It will be nothing but a time and energy drain for all involved. The cure becomes the disease, and it is ruining the principalship, not to mention student learning itself. In addition, the entire premise is individualistic. There is nothing in the strategy about developing the group. It's as if the system has unlimited supervisory capacity and that principals have all the time in the world to change teachers one at a time.

Large-scale compliance diktats minimize impact—just the opposite of what is intended. To be clear, there are good ideas in the SGO document, but they cannot be fulfilled by compliance-driven specificity. The goodness gets squandered as principals and teachers find themselves going through the contortions of compliance or the distortions of defiance. Far better to set the conditions for maximizing impact that I describe in this book, whereby principals and teachers are helped to develop their professional capital and corresponding expertise and commitments, and then scrutinize for quality and accountability, all in a transparent manner. As Kirtman (2013) found about effective leaders, they are low on compliance for the sake of compliance, and high on influence for the sake of learning. They influence others to learn and to take related action. Commitment always trumps compliance as a change strategy.

My conclusion is that neither school autonomy nor detailed observations are effective in producing results at scale. Instead we need a model that is still intense in its focus on instruction but that also involves and motivates *all teachers*.

# Time to Retune

Given the urgency of the need for reform, we are rapidly losing ground relative to a problem that has severe consequences for society: the gap between high and low performers in the education system. In addition to the facts that the counter-productive strategies we've discussed in this chapter are really barriers that make the principal's job more difficult, erode the energy and commitment of principals (thereby squandering the second most powerful impact factor for student learning), and simply do not work. The further irony is that these barriers make the role of school principals way more complicated than it needs to be, loading them with one big bundle of distracters that render the job unsustainable. As I noted in Chapter One, 75 percent of principals find that the job has become too complex, and thereby unsatisfying. Principals cannot be effective under these circumstances. We have taken instructional leadership too literally or have chased the dream of individual heroic leaders working autonomously to save the day.

This need not be the case, and the good news is that ideas are emerging that could make the principal's job less complex, less distracting, and yes, more instructionally effective for all. This chapter has been long on vices and short on virtues. It is time to change the channel. A new, more powerful role—that of the principal as lead learner—is becoming clear. The next chapter lays out this exciting and efficacious new direction.

# Action Items

☐ Has any change at your school gotten off on the wrong foot or gone in the wrong direction? How did that happen?

☐ Have decisions in your district been driven recently by accountability, individualistic solutions, technology, or fragmented policies/strategies? What driver(s) might have been better?

☐ Does too much of your time go to micromanagement? Why?

☐ Are you in the right place between the broad and narrow paths? What steps can you take to get to the right place?

# Discuss with Colleagues

- What vicious circles do we see in our daily work? What virtuous ones?

- How can we keep up a sense of urgency that leads to right decisions and productive change?

- How can we steer clear of micromanagement?

- How has our school district been affected by the movements for instructional leadership or transformational leadership, or by school autonomy options?

# CHAPTER · THREE

# The First Key—
# Leading Learning

I n Chapter Two, we saw that the principalship is hard enough, yet we have made it more complicated than it has to be. Principals are spending more and more time on instruction, but it is not time well spent, in that it does not yield widespread results. To increase impact, principals should use their time differently. They should direct their energies to developing the group. This does not exclude the role of selecting and cultivating individuals, but it places that activity within the context of creating a collective culture of efficacy.

As I've mentioned earlier, we can call this first role "leading learning," "learning leader," or "lead learner." Hierarchical leadership can never influence the masses on any scale, but purposeful peers can have this effect. So the principal's role is to lead the school's teachers in a process of learning to improve their teaching, while learning alongside them about what works and what doesn't. The nature of this new, much more powerful leadership role is becoming increasingly clear. In this chapter, I capture what research tells us about this more effective leadership role, and then furnish a framework that will guide the principal to maximize impact on teacher and student learning.

I start by surveying key research findings into what effective principals do that yield results in leading learning. Second, I describe a framework for seeing one's school in terms of its "professional capital." The final section offers some ways for principals to center the lead learner aspects of their practice. Throughout, we will be asking whether what we find can be executed on a large scale, not just here and there.

# What Key Research Tells Us

I begin with less than a handful of studies that best identify the core work of the principal as learning leader. With this core work in mind, I will discuss the work of leading learning in terms of the gathering and spending of three forms of professional capital.

Although I don't directly take up the "managerial" role of the principal, let me say here that for the professional agenda to flourish, the principal must ensure that good management prevails in the school. One way I have expressed this is that leaders need to address and contend with "distractors"—events and issues that take the school away from focusing on the core learning priorities. Effective leaders maintain focus, as I have found in my motion leadership case studies of specific leaders (Fullan, 2013a). Lead learner principals are wary of taking on too many innovations; they avoid the allure of more money and high-profile initiatives. They make sure that the basics—budget, timetable, health, and safety—are addressed effectively. Drawing distinctions between leadership and management has never appealed to me. In fact, leading the development of a culture of professional capital requires strong *managerial* skills. The skill set that is the basis of Chapter Five is about effective leadership per se—no need to artificially sort out what is managerial and what is leadership.

The distinction some like to draw between managers and leaders that casts the latter as visionaries is a vague, romantic notion of the transformational leader. Show me a transformational leader who is not a good manager, and I will show you a failed organization—glitzy for a while, but inevitably giving change a bad name. Lead learners are very good managers, because they know that establishing basic routines is essential for improvement goals to succeed. In short, principals must ensure that basic managerial functions are carried out effectively, which will entail delegating these aspects (but under their auspices). The fact remains, however, that the administrative and improvement burden has dramatically increased for principals over the past decade, and, as I said in the last chapter, some of that work includes needless time wasters (such as tedious, superficial appraisal). Principals do need better support. A new role of school manager in large schools is also emerging, but again, this role should be within the principal's purview. In other words, the principal should not be expected to do everything, but should ensure that key tasks are done well—what CEO does not have a managerial team?

> , , ,

A ton has been written on the role of the principal as it affects student learning, but I am going to look at four authors and their teams of colleagues who have examined the role in detail over the last three decades: Viviane Robinson, Helen Timperley, Ken Leithwood, and Tony Bryk. Their findings are consistent: principals affect student learning *indirectly but nonetheless explicitly*. To that distinguished group, I'll add Lyle Kirtman and his work on leadership and teams.

### Viviane Robinson: Lead Learner as the Key Domain

Viviane Robinson and her colleagues conducted a large-scale "best evidence synthesis" (BES) of research on the impact of school principals on student achievement. Robinson summarizes their conclusions in a book titled *Student-Centered Leadership* (2011). She found five leadership domains that had significant effect sizes (shown in parentheses) on student achievement:

1. Establishing goals and expectations (0.42)
2. Resourcing strategically (0.31)
3. Ensuring quality teaching (0.42)
4. Leading teacher learning and development (0.84)
5. Ensuring an orderly and safe environment (0.27)

There are specific dos and don'ts within each category, but the message they carry as a set is quite clear. The most significant factor—twice as powerful as any other—is "leading teacher learning and development," which is essentially what I mean by the role of learning leader. Within item 4, Robinson found that the principal who makes the biggest impact on learning is the one who attends to other matters as well, but, most important, "participates as a learner" with teachers in helping move the school forward. Leading teacher learning means being proactively involved with teachers such that principal and teachers alike are learning.

Think of it this way: the principal who covers only such areas as establishing a vision, acquiring resources for teachers, working to help individual teachers, and other similar activities does not necessarily *learn* what is specifically needed to stimulate ongoing organizational improvement. For the latter to happen, the principal must make both teacher learning and his or her own learning a priority. Within this domain of teacher learning and development, Robinson found two critical factors: the ability of the principal to make progress a collective endeavor (a core theme of this book), and skills for leading professional learning. To extrapolate from Robinson, both of these factors require the principal to be present as a learner. Principals who do not take the learner *stance* for themselves do not learn much from day to day, no matter how many years of "experience" they may accumulate, as little of that prior experience was really aimed at their own *learning*. Thus principals need to chart their own learning and be aware of its curve from day one if they are going to get better at leading. And they do this best through helping teachers learn. We have found this to be especially true in our work in the "new pedagogies" (learning partnerships between and among teachers using technology to accelerate and deepen learning; Fullan & Langworthy, 2014). Principals who visibly struggle with new digital devices in their own learning, who seek to learn from students and teachers about new technologies, who, in short, put themselves on the learning line, are very much appreciated in the school. And, of course, they learn more and become better able to assist teachers.

Robinson also identified what she called three key "leadership capabilities" that cut across the five domains:

1. Applying relevant knowledge
2. Solving complex problems
3. Building relational trust

Combined, the five leadership domains and the three capabilities encompass a pretty tight characterization of the lead learner at work.

## Helen Timperley: "Who Is My Class?"

Helen Timperley, Robinson's colleague at the University of Auckland and also a longtime researcher of the role of principal and of teacher learning, conducted a parallel BES study on teacher learning—in other words, examining research on the relationship between teacher learning and student achievement. In her book *Realizing the Power of Professional Learning* (2011), she drew similar conclusions:

> Coherence across professional learning environments was not achieved through the completion of checklists and scripted lessons but rather through creating learning situations that promoted inquiry habits of mind throughout the school. (p. 104)

Timperley comes up with the wonderful question for principals: "Who is my class?" One principal noted that she and other principals were so busy attending to the needs of the individual teachers that they didn't attend to the leadership learning needs of team leaders. This principal concluded that "her class" of learners included team leaders who in turn can leverage the learning of other teachers in their group, thereby generating greater learning across the school.

## Ken Leithwood: Skills, Motivation, and Working Conditions

Ken Leithwood at the University of Toronto, Karen Seashore Louis at Minnesota, and their colleagues have become masters of the principalship over the last four decades. In their book *Linking Leadership to Student Learning*, Leithwood and Seashore Louis (2012) conclude that principals who had the greatest impact on student learning in the school focused on instruction—including teacher knowledge, skills, motivation—and on ensuring supportive working conditions (such as time for collaboration). Putting it in a nutshell, they say that "leadership affects student learning when it is targeted at working relationships, improving instruction and, indirectly, student achievement" (p. 234). Note that as I mentioned earlier, the impact on student learning is not direct, but is nonetheless explicit. The causal pathways are not vague, as they are in transformational leadership, but rather are made explicit, sometimes by the principal but more often by coaches, other teacher leaders, and peers—*orchestrated by hands-on principals*. This is a theme we will see time and again. We will return to Leithwood in Chapter Four when we consider the relationship of the school to the district.

### Tony Bryk: Capacity, Climate, Community, Instruction

As president of the Carnegie Foundation for the Advancement of Teaching, Tony Bryk is leading work on bringing researchers and practitioners together to improve teaching and learning. Bryk and his colleagues' longitudinal research in the 477 elementary schools in Chicago is especially informative for our purposes (Bryk, Bender-Sebring, Allensworth, Lupescu, & Easton, 2010). In a microcosm comparison of two schools that started out at similar levels of low performance, one school (called Hancock) improved significantly over a six-year period, compared to another (called Alexander). The difference:

> Strong principal leadership at Hancock School fostered the development of a vigorous professional community that was both actively reaching out to parents and sustaining a focus on

improving instruction. In contrast, reform efforts at Alexander remained fragmented, suffering from both poor coordination and a lack of follow through. (p. 40)

There were major reform activities at both schools (recall Kotter's frenetic urgency versus focused urgency). But Alexander actually lost ground in reading by 9 percent and made no improvement in math over the years, whereas Hancock gained 10 percent in reading and 19 percent in math. Here I've mentioned just two schools, but fortunately Bryk and colleagues have data on nearly all of the 477 elementary schools in Chicago.

When we consider the comprehensive picture, comparing, as Bryk et al. (2010) did, the hundred or so schools that made significant progress to their peer schools that did not progress, we see what should now be a familiar picture. The key explanation was "school leadership as the driver for change" (p. 62), which in turn focused on the development of four interrelated forces: the professional capacity of teachers (individually and collectively), school climate (ensuring safety and orderliness in the aid of learning), parent and community ties, and what the researchers call the "instructional guidance system" (instructional practices that engage students in relation to key learning goals) as these affected each and every classroom (p. 62). This is quite a compact list of what effective school leaders focus on. The problem is that Bryk et al. found these elements in only about one hundred schools, less than 20 percent of the total. Our goal is "whole-system change" in which 100 percent of the schools are positively affected.

⸙ ⸙ ⸙

Despite the consistency of these findings from this sample of leading researchers, the message is not getting across or sticking with those involved in developing school leadership. Success at the school level is a function of the work of principals, themselves acting as lead learners, who ensure that the group focuses on a small number of key elements: specific goals for students; data that enable clear diagnosis of individual learning needs; instructional practices that address those learning needs; and teachers learning from each other, monitoring overall progress, and making adjustments accordingly. All of this is carried out in a developmental climate (as distinct from a judgmental one) with norms of transparency within and external to the school. Within this set of conditions, accountability measures, including teacher evaluation, can and do occur, but they are conducted within a culture of collaborative improvement.

Despite the clarity and consistency of these findings—over decades now—it is still seemingly easy for well-intentioned school leaders and those shaping the principalship to get it wrong—to err badly along the lines of the problems I identified in Chapter Two, namely, use the wrong drivers, shortcut the process through weak individualistic solutions, become too broad or too narrow, and make deals with the devil by opting for school autonomy. We need to push a little deeper on the underlying meaning of this consistent work in order to make it stick.

## Lyle Kirtman—Content and Organization

In *Change Leader: Learning to Do What Matters Most* (2011), I made the case that practice drives theory better than the other way around. This is why I like Lyle Kirtman's new book, *Leadership and Teams* (2013). Applying his management consultancy perspective (having worked with several hundred public and private sector organizations over the course of thirty years), Lyle dug directly into school leadership practice by finding out from over six hundred education leaders what competencies (observable behaviors or skills) were associated with effectiveness. By examining what high-performing leaders actually did in practice to get results, Kirtman found that these leaders possessed seven competencies—qualities, incidentally, that are quite congruent with my "motion leadership" study of how leaders "move" individuals and organizations forward (Fullan, 2013a). Chapter Five takes up Kirtman's full set of seven competencies in detail, but of direct interest to us here is what he confirms about leaders and instruction:

> The role of the principal needs to be balanced between content and organizational leadership. These competencies involve building instructional leadership into the culture of the school and building strong leadership in teachers. The educational leader is the overall leader of instruction, but he or she needs to have time and skills to motivate and build teams and develop leadership capacity in his or her school for change. *The educational leader should try not to do too much on his or her own in the instructional arena.* (Kirtman, 2013, p. 8, emphasis added)

It is understandable that some people misinterpret the emphasis on the instructional leadership of the principal. They mistakenly assume that instructional leadership means that principals must spend much of their time in classrooms working *directly* with individual teachers. The findings about effectiveness that I have reviewed in this chapter are not telling us that the best principals spend several days a week in classrooms, but that they do enough of it regularly to maintain and develop their instructional expertise. It is not that they affect very many teachers one by one, but that they work with other leaders in the school and together affect teachers more in groups than they do individually. (We will come back to the topic of individual teacher appraisal in the next section, under "Human and Social Capital.")

Kirtman says that "school leaders are being told to focus on instructional leadership[,] . . . narrow their initiatives to implement particular programs, and . . . are being told that teachers must be evaluated with stronger, more airtight forms and processes in order to weed out the poor teachers" (p. 45). With this kind of approach, an autocratic principal can extract short-term results, but in the course of doing this will alienate teachers (including or maybe especially the best ones) and will never be able to generate in teachers the motivation and ingenuity for them to be able to go the extra mile. Programs will come and go, as will individual principals. Little worthwhile will stick.

## The Punch Line

Before getting to my own preferred solution—the development of professional capital in teachers—let me summarize the core meaning of the findings just reviewed. First, this body of research establishes that groups of teachers, working together in purposeful ways over periods of time, will produce greater learning in more students. Thus, if principals directly influence how teachers can learn together, they will maximize their impact on student learning.

Second, although the route to impacting student achievement is one step removed, causally speaking, it must be nonetheless explicit. If principals merely enable teachers to work together and do not help forge the final link to actual learning, the process will fail. Let me illustrate this using a study of professional learning communities (PLCs) in two districts. The researchers were Caryn M. Wells, a former principal now on the educational leadership faculty at Oakland University (OU, Minnesota), and her OU colleague, Lindson Feun. Wells and Feun (2013) studied the implementation of PLCs in two sets of four middle schools in two districts (called Districts A and B) with comparable demographics. The two districts were similar in terms of teacher responses to such items as "agreement about the need to collaborate" and "agreement about what should be a learning community," but there were big differences when it came to the specifics— particularly with respect to making explicit links to student learning. On questions pertaining to whether "teachers examine and compare student learning results," "teachers discuss instructional methods used to teach students," and "seek new teaching methods, testing and reflecting on results," District A had mean responses on a 5-point scale in the 2.17 to 2.44 range, whereas District B responses were in the 3.19 to 3.70 range.

In short, schools in District B more intensely focused on the things that would most directly and specifically affect instruction and achievement. School leaders worked with teachers to develop their capacity to work with data analysis linked to the personalized learning needs of students. It was this focus and precision that distinguished the two districts. And District B, as would be expected, showed evidence of "raised student achievement" (p. 253). The key to generating widespread impact on student learning then, resides in mobilizing the group to work in specific, intense, sustained ways on learning for all students. We have seen that this work involves teachers working together to examine individual student progress, decide on and implement best instructional responses, learn from each other what is working, and build on what they are learning.

I have said that the message about leading collaborative groups is not getting through despite years of consistent evidence. In an effort to make this work more focused, I offer a framework in the next section through which we can make this learning solution systemic.

## Professional Capital—a Framework for Leading Learning

So, how to be a leader of learning? In my work with the government in Ontario since 2003, which I cited in Chapter Two, our core strategy was to invest in capacity building with a focus on student results. What we did was develop the capacity of leaders to foster focused collaborative work within and across schools and districts. In effect, this work has turned out to be a precursor to the more fundamental and comprehensive concept of professional capital, which my co-conspirator Andy Hargreaves of the Lynch School of Education, Boston College, and I coined and developed in *Professional Capital: Transforming Teaching in Every School* (2012) as a framework for radically improving the teaching profession.

Let's begin with an example of aspects of the professional capital concept in action. We filmed Park Manor Public School in Elmira, Ontario, because it was producing great results in student achievement using well-directed collaborative strategies that employed technology to dramatically improve proficiency in reading and writing. In the following passage, Park Manor's principal, James Bond, describes how he supports innovation as he helps teachers across the school learn to be more effective in employing technology:

> You need to be willing to get messy, as every tool, program, application or website will not work perfectly every time and the beginning is inefficient . . . I tried to make it easy for teachers by having it in their classrooms set up for them all the time, so they just have to turn it on . . . Especially in the beginning when there wasn't much expertise in the school, I would showcase and model applications at staff meetings or professional development sessions. We used the gradual release model and differentiated the professional development each teacher needed based on their zone of proximal learning.
>
> I was also willing to help them when they had problems, so they would be ok with not knowing how to use it in front of me and see that it was ok not to know how to use it perfectly . . .
>
> As more expertise grew in the building, I encouraged the staff to learn from each other and then even from the students. I really tried to connect teachers who were learning how to use technology to those teachers who were reluctant . . . I really tried to let the staff find ways . . . to help their students and let go of other uses that they weren't ready for or didn't feel were value added, although I could see the benefits. (Personal communication, May 2013)

At the school, we watched Bond being quite explicit about fostering learning among staff—learning that develops "exemplary pedagogy" (the school's term) that promotes improved learning in such difficult domains as critical thinking, communication, and problem solving. The teachers confirmed the daily presence of these strategies. For example, said one teacher, "James allowed collaboration time with other 'informed' staff members—shared apps, sites, and tips with us technologically inept individuals." Bond practiced and encouraged "'on the fly' sharing of 'how to' websites" and other suggestions. He emphasized "having the technology available to the students so we could learn alongside them."

Another teacher noted that "James allowed us to explore technology at our own pace . . . did not push it on us. He encouraged those who were comfortable with new uses and applications to share their successes with us, which in turn, made some of us try."

A third responded positively to Bond's "adding a section to the learning cycle template that included how to use technology ([it] got me thinking about how I was going to integrate technology from the beginning of the planning cycle)." Bond pointed the teacher toward "asking students how they like to use different technologies and have them show me how to use it (if I did not already know)." He also got "other teachers to show me how they use technology (i.e. staff meeting when we went to everyone's room)."

As Bond's example should suggest, the actions of the principal as leading learning, the way in which he or she expects and enables staff to learn from each other in specific ways that develop their capacities and that enhance student learning, are all manifestations of professional capital at work. Being a good change leader, Bond creates a nonjudgmental climate (it's OK to make mistakes as you learn). The culture of the school is the focal point for all of its staff and students. As this collaborative learning culture becomes embedded, it becomes less and less dependent on the actions of the principal and more a function of how staff carry on their day-to-day work, and how everyone learns from each other. The end result is that the principal and the teachers, as a group, are in this together. It is no accident that students' proficiency scores on the province's high-standard assessment increased from 72 percent to 93 percent in reading and from 70 percent to 87 percent in writing in the first three years of this work.

The work at Park Manor reflects what Hargreaves and I call professional capital, which we see as the key to diffusing change efforts from individuals to groups to schools and districts. Professional capital is a function of the interaction of three components: human capital, social capital, and decisional capital. In the principal's case, *human capital* refers to the human resource or personnel dimension of the quality of teachers in the school—their basic teaching talents. Recruiting and cultivating the skills of individual teachers is one dimension of the principal's role. *Social capital* concerns the quality and quantity of interactions and relationships among people. Social capital in a school affects teachers' access to knowledge and information; their sense of expectation, obligation, and trust; and their commitment to work together for a common cause. *Decisional (or decision-making) capital* refers to the sum of practice and expertise in making decisions across many individuals or groups within a school and its community. Decisional capital is that which is required to make good decisions—specific decisions, as we shall see, about how to put human and social capital to work for achieving the goals of the school.

This three-part conception of professional capital can be used as a way of organizing the principal's roles in leading learning. In effect, the role of school leaders is to build professional capital across and beyond the school. All three components must be addressed explicitly and in combination.

### Human and Social Capital

When human and social capital are combined, they produce powerful outcomes. We see one clear example of this phenomenon in the work of Carrie Leana (2011), a management professor at University of Pittsburg with strong credentials in learning research. She claims as I do here that commonly touted change strategies typically err in trusting too much in the power of individuals to solve educational problems, while failing to enlist and capitalize on the power of the group. Just hire great teachers and great principals, and the problem will be solved.

In a straightforward study of elementary schools in New York City, Leana measured only three main variables:

- **Human capital**—by gathering information on the classroom experience and qualifications of individual teachers
- **Social capital**—by asking such questions as, "To what extent do you work with other teachers in the school in a focused collaborative way to improve learning for students?"
- **Math achievement** over a one-year period

Although Leana did find that teachers with greater human capital yielded greater math results, the teachers who achieved the greatest gains for their students were good at math teaching *and* worked with peers regularly to improve what they were doing and what they could learn from each other. She also found that teachers with lower skills who happened to be working in a school with high social capital got better results. In the worst scenario, both human and social capital were low.

Human capital should not be thought of as the main driver to develop the school. Although it's true that in situations where teacher quality is extremely low, bringing in great leaders (high individual human capital) is essential for beginning a turnaround process, little meaningful change results unless and until social capital enables the group to get its act together. Once you get started, social capital (the group) improves individuals more readily than individuals improve the group. For example, it is actually very hard for a weak teacher who enters a highly collaborative school to remain there without improving. Conversely, a highly talented individual will not remain in a non-collaborative school for very long. To paraphrase the post–World War I hit about Paris: How you gonna keep 'em down on the farm, after they've seen *the farm?!* Good people will not stay in places that are unproductive.

Ultimately, we need both human and social capital, and we need the group to change the group for the better. The principal who spends a lot of time at the individual level, as current strategies demand, has less time to spend fostering group work and thereby building social capital with and among teachers and with the community and other sources of external support. How is the following for a finding?

When principals spent more time building external social capital [with the community, and seeking other sources of ideas], the quality of instruction in the school was higher and students' scores on standardized tests in both reading and math were higher. Conversely, principals spending more of their time mentoring and monitoring teachers had no effect on teacher social capital or student achievement. The more effective principals were those who defined their role as *facilitators* of teacher success rather than instructional leaders. They provided teachers with the resources they needed to build social capital—time, space, and staffing—to make the informal and formal connections possible. (Leana, 2011, p. 35, emphasis in original)

Let's not misinterpret the direction that these findings are taking us. The implication is not that principals should abandon the focus on instruction, but rather that they should get at it by working with teachers individually and collectively to develop *their* professional capital. The press for continuous instructional improvement is central. There is still a lot of precision to be had—what specific expertise is needed for learning in math; what teams are needed for what tasks; what is the new pedagogy that enlists students as partners in learning and uses technology to accelerate and deepen learning. The principal is in there by helping the group get that good. The question is, what combination of factors will maximize that press for most teachers' learning and therefore for most students' learning?

Schools that invest in both human and social capital and make them interact build the resources required for schoolwide success. They quite simply come to have the wherewithal to accomplish wider and deeper results. The principal's role is to participate as a learner and leader in ensuring that the combined human and social capital forces are devoted to outcomes in a targeted, continuous manner.

**Attracting and improving human capital**

Human capital is essentially about the quality of individual teachers—the personnel dimension, if you will. It depends on attracting and then cultivating talent. Not all principals have the choice of who is on staff, but the front-end task is to hire teachers who have at least four core qualities: (1) high moral commitment relative to the learning of *all students* regardless of background, (2) strong instructional practice, (3) desire to work collaboratively, and (4) commitment to continuous learning. Even if some of these qualities are wanting at the outset, it is the principal's job to foster them once people are hired—again using strategies to develop both human and social capital.

Thus further development on the job is the key. We know that most teachers do not receive ongoing feedback about the quality of their teaching. The question then is, what conditions or processes best serve that purpose? I have already observed that formal appraisal schemes represent a crude and ineffective method as *the main mechanism* for giving constructive feedback. How many professions do you know in which formal appraisal looms as the major instrument of improvement? There are better ways of improving all teachers and of getting rid of the bottom 5 percent—one of them being the building of a strong collaborative culture (in other words, social capital). If you make developing the culture the main strategy, formal feedback becomes a lot easier. Thus much of the effective feedback becomes built into the day-to-day purposeful interactions of the culture at work. And recall that the effective principal participates in shaping the culture of learning. Cultures are organic and, by definition, persistent, and consequently are more effective in influencing their members. Most teachers want constructive feedback to get better, and most find it lacking in the culture of their profession.

In my experience, formal appraisal schemes always become counterproductive when people bend over backwards to separate coaching from "evaluation"—for example, by specifying that instructional coaches should give only nonevaluative feedback or by making principals responsible only for formal, consequential evaluation. This separation typically is associated with *low-trust cultures*. It's there to protect. But put all the protective mechanisms you want in a low-trust culture, and you will still never achieve motivated development. All feedback in a sense is evaluative, and when delivered *primarily for growth*, it results in improvement. If the main point is to provide feedback that is acted on, and surely it should be, then let's see how that can be accomplished best, and not make formal appraisal an end in itself.

In all of the literature about principals who lead successful schools, one factor comes up time and again: *relational trust*. When it comes to growth, relational trust pertains to feelings that the culture supports continuous learning rather than early judgments about how weak or strong you might be. Principals who help build collaborative cultures do so by establishing conditions of nonjudgmentalism (by offering feedback primarily for growth) and transparency (by being open about results and about practice). Most teachers grow under these conditions, and in a culture of healthy pressure (high expectations), and support (both technical and emotional), peers help each other grow. When these dynamics are under way, principals are in a better position to take action relative to persistently ineffective teachers (who indeed become few in number). In fact, Bryk and Schneider (2002) found that principals who had high relational trust with teachers as a group were more likely to act to dismiss incompetent teachers—an act that was appreciated by staff as a whole; in high-performing groups, peers don't like members who don't pull their own weight.

The key questions in this section are what attracts quality people to join a profession or an organization, and what makes them become more effective on the job. The historical problem is that teachers actually receive very little feedback about their work—a problem that is still predominant today. In its Teaching and Learning International Survey of teachers in twenty-five countries, the Organisation for Economic Co-operation and Development (OECD, 2013) strikes an all-too-familiar note: 22 percent of the teachers have *never* had any feedback from their principals (not to mention whether the feedback was valuable for any of those who did get appraised); over 50 percent have never received feedback from an external source; yet 79 percent of teachers would find constructive feedback helpful.

So, no feedback is obviously unacceptable. But the justification for leaping from that situation to positioning teacher evaluation as *the solution* has no basis in evidence. In a recent blog post, Marc Tucker (2013), the head of the National Center for Education and the Economy, posed the following true-or-false question: "Teacher evaluations improve accountability, raise achievement." He found no evidence that the implementation of teacher evaluation at scale produces significant improvements in student performance. Tucker observed, "I know of no successful system for managing professionals anywhere in the world that relies for its success mainly on getting rid of poor performers to meet its quality targets."

As I've already stated, formal teacher appraisal is a crude instrument that by itself can never produce the intended results. When systems insist that their principals engage in appraisal for all teachers, they place these principals on a treadmill of pointless activity (to borrow a phrase from a recent *Economist* in talking about unnecessary meetings). Good principals know this and either leave the profession or go through the motions (what I referred to earlier as the cat joining the mice). The solution is almost commonsensical. What is likely to produce better feedback for improvement: episodic superficial feedback, or working alongside colleagues engaged in improvement day after day? You can use both—teacher evaluation and collaborative cultures—just get the order right.

As to the appraisal system itself, make it more directly helpful for growth along the following lines (see also the framework from the Australian Institute for Teaching and School Leadership, 2012):

1. **Make the appraisal framework sound** (based on best standards and efficient ways of assessing them).

2. **Underpin its use with a philosophy oriented to development and improvement rather than with an evaluative punitive stance.**

3. **Make the learning culture of schools and districts the main event and integrate any performance appraisal such that it serves this shared work.**

4. **Ensure that professional development and learning are fundamental, ongoing features of the entire process.**

5. **Realize that by far the most effective and telling feedback that teachers will receive is that which is built into the purposeful interaction between and among teachers and the principal.** Such interaction is specific to the task of learning. For example, collective analysis of evidence of student learning and the practices that lead to greater learning is at the heart of continuous improvement.

In short, use formal appraisal of your human capital to buttress the work of day-to-day improvement, but integrate it into group work.

### Social capital

As I suggested earlier, social capital is expressed in the interactions and relationships that support a common cause among the staff of any school. There is no question that a group with plenty of social capital is able to accomplish much more than a group with little—and this is not a correlation but cause and effect. Interpersonal trust and individual expertise work hand in hand toward better results. Social capital increases an individual's knowledge because it gives him or her access to other people's human capital.

Absence of social capital helps explain why professional development often does not have much effect. Peter Cole (2004) was formerly with the Victoria (Australia) Department of Education and Training, and is now a consultant who focuses on professional learning. Who could not be intrigued by the title of his article, "Professional Development: A Great Way to

Avoid Change," in which he describes how people go to work-shops, feel as though they are learning something new, and then rarely follow through. Of course what matters is what happens after (or between) workshops: Who tries things out? Who supports you? Who gives you feedback? Who picks you up when you make a mistake? Who else can you learn from? How can you take responsibility for change together? Productive answers to all these questions depend on the culture to which one returns, and especially on its social capital. Cole's paper "Aligning Professional Learning, Performance Management and Effective Teaching" (2013) draws conclusions similar to those in the case I am making here: the culture of the school and the district must be the main focus.

Thus a principal's main role is to build the social capital of teachers working together—and this is quite precise work in relation to improving the learning of students, consisting of specific attention to personalized learning, diagnosis of learning needs, instruction that suits the purpose, and teachers' learning from each other what works best. It is also crucial to build the social capital of the broader community. Especially in those schools situated in communities with severely deprived conditions, it is essential for the school to reach out and develop ties with parents and community leaders. Bryk et al. (2010) put it this way:

> Herbie Hancock Elementary School succeeded despite its location in a high-crime neighborhood with weak social resources. It is a story of exceptional leadership that created strong links with organizations both inside and outside the community, and built relational trust among school community members, while pursuing a program of improvement. (p. 195)

Both Bryk et al. (2010) and Leithwood (2011) show that on a larger scale—multiple schools—developing the social capital of schools and that of the community forms a powerful combination. When schools work on their own social capital, they are more likely to see parents and the community as part of the solution; when they remain isolated individualistic cultures, they can easily treat parents as part of the problem, thereby reinforcing a downward spiral.

## Decisional Capital

As I noted earlier, decisional capital refers to resources of knowledge, intelligence, and energy that are required to put human and social capital to effective use. It is, basically, the capacity to choose well and make good decisions. It is best thought of as expertise that grows over time. It also should be thought of at both the level of the individual (that is, a given teacher's expertise) and the level of the group (the collective judgment of two or more teachers). Like decision making itself, the process of accumulating decisional capital should also be deliberate. In schools, principals must have great decisional capital of their own, but even more of it should reside in the many other individuals and the groups that schools comprise. When the decision-making skills of individuals and group decision making feed on each other, professional judgment in the school as a whole becomes more powerful.

This would be a good time to take up the recent interest in "instructional rounds," first introduced by Elizabeth City, Richard Elmore, Sarah Fiarman, and Lee Teitel (2009) of Harvard. "Rounds," as it is called, is a new practice that is intended to help educators look closely at (observe) learning and teaching in their classrooms so that they can work together to improve it. The first instances of this practice involved administrators—superintendents and principals. I would say that the value of this first manifestation of rounds was for the professional learning of administrators, not as a strategy for actual improvement. Participating administrators learned a great deal—many of them have not been that close to the class-room for a while—but the procedure is too far removed from day-to-day planning to make a difference.

In further work, the group, led by Teitel (2013), has developed a more grounded version of school-based instructional rounds. This strategy increases the agency of teachers. Rather than just being observed, teachers become involved in observing and analyzing others. The frequency of observation is also increased. As Teitel states, "by conducting more frequent, smaller, shorter-term improvement cycles through school-based rounds, instructional improvements can be implemented and fine-tuned more regularly, with potentially speedier impacts and a greater sense of teacher and school-based efficacy" (p. 3). This work is certainly in the wheelhouse of professional capital. It shifts the center of gravity from top-down compliance to teacher engagement and collective efficacy. My best advice, though, is to remember that "rounds" is just a tool or a program at best. There is no substitute for a collaborative culture that builds in learning every day. Use rounds if this helps to extend your learning; use it as a complement to your instructional learning, but not as an answer to the more basic task of establishing a shared culture that continually addresses and solves specific problems of students.

We have come full circle. Working in isolation obviously does not increase professional expertise on any scale. Nor does working together automatically increase it. Beware of schools where teachers appear to be working together but mainly run on "contrived collegiality," where administrators have mandated PLCs or "cozy collaboration," in which there is little focus and intensity of effort, as was the case in District A of our PLC example discussed earlier in this chapter (Wells & Feun, 2013).

Instead, decisional capital is developed as part and parcel of learning cultures. Consider this example from outside the field of education. Liker and Meier (2007), who have studied Toyota over the years, found that Toyota's culture, because it focused on both individual and group learning, was very effective at getting great results. The authors traced this strength to "the depth of understanding among Toyota's employees regarding their work" (p. 112). I prefer to say *shared depth*. You don't get depth at a workshop; you don't get it just by hiring great individuals; you don't get it just through evaluations. And you don't get it through congenial relationships. You develop shared depth through continuous learning, by solving problems, and by getting better and better at what you do. Developing expertise day after day by making learning and its impact the focus of the work is what pays off. Expertise, individual and collective, is what counts.

In schools and educational systems, decisional capital is about cultivating human and social capital over time, deliberately identifying and spreading the instructional practices that are most effective for meeting the learning goals of the school. People don't learn these practices once and for all in pre-service teacher education programs. They learn them best by practicing on the job and having access to coaches and skilled peers. In education, as in any profession, leaders need to make discretionary decisions so as to respond effectively to the situation at hand. When a teacher has to consult the manual or check the scripted lesson to address a parent's difficult question, you know that the teacher is not a professional.

Hargreaves and I took our idea of decisional capital from case law, though we might have arrived at it by following doctors on medical rounds. Yes, there are precedents one can follow, but professionals become truly expert only to the extent that they can make a wise decision when no precedent tells them what to do. Alongside partners, associates, mentors, and team members, they attempt to resolve cases or defeat diseases that can't always be found in a reference book. Over time, they become skilled at judging (diagnosing) what is needed, and they respond effectively more frequently. They learn to become better judges and physicians.

When the school is organized to focus on a small number of shared goals, and when professional learning is targeted to those goals and is a collective enterprise, the evidence is overwhelming that teachers can do dramatically better by way of student achievement. Well-led school-based learning with peers is the best way to learn the fundamentals of teachings—let's call them the nonnegotiable basics. When University of Melbourne education researcher John Hattie (2009) conducted his in-depth research synthesis of over eight hundred meta-analyses, he did us a favor by identifying the high-impact teaching practices. These practices—such as giving feedback to students, frequently examining the effects of teaching, encouraging metacognition whereby students become self-aware and in greater control of their own learning, establishing peer learning among students, and so on—are best learned explicitly and with peers.

But what about reaching the expert decisional level, where deeper judgment is required? For example, how might you help a sullen student discover what might be his interests, or his "element," as Sir Ken Robinson (2013) advises? How can you sharpen the critical thinking skills of students? And so on. Teachers can become experts along these lines or not depending largely on whether they are in a collaborative school; teachers, including potentially good teachers, can also exit the profession early when they are stifled by individualistic cultures. And whether they become decisional experts has a great deal to do with the quality of leadership they experience. Hattie (2012) asks,

> Think of reasons why a teacher would stay in teaching . . . The factor that explains the decision to stay or not—by a long way—relates to the nature of leadership . . . It is leaders' . . . identifying and articulating high expectations for all, consulting with teachers before making decisions that affect teachers, fostering communication, allocating resources, developing organizational structures to support instruction and learning, and regularly collecting and reviewing with teachers data on student learning. Learning leadership is the most powerful incentive to stay in teaching. (p.153)

Expert teachers, says Hattie, "can provide defensible evidence of positive impacts of the teaching on student learning" (2012, p. 24). One becomes this good through deliberate practice on a continuous basis, which can be done on one's own, but is much more likely to occur if forcefully led and accelerated by the group. The best way to foster expertise at scale is to use the group to change the group. The role of the principal in this endeavor is clear: it is to help establish challenging goals and "safe environments for teachers to critique, question, and support other teachers to reach these goals together. These are the leaders who have most effect on student outcomes" (Hattie, 2009, p. 83).

In one of his best sellers, *Outliers*, Malcolm Gladwell (2008) made the ten-thousand-hour rule famous. That figure comes up time and again for individuals trying to become accomplished at their trade: ten thousand hours of "deliberate practice" over ten years or more. It is what separates professionals from the rest of us. I suppose that it is obvious that this process can be accelerated when people are learning from each other, and that, equally, it may never succeed (except for the odd genius) if a person simply goes it alone. Some guitarists go on playing the same three chords their entire lives, not seeking higher knowledge of music. Similarly, teaching is not the kind of profession where staying cloistered will often bring one to personal mastery or end up having much collective impact.

So it is practice at exercising judgment, and a great deal of it, that accumulates one's decisional capital. And power of judgment is sharpened and accelerated when it is mediated through learning with colleagues (social capital). High-yield strategies become more precise and more embedded when they are developed and deployed in teams that are constantly refining and interpreting them according to their impact on students across the school. Even when clear evidence is lacking or conflicting, accumulated collective experience carries much more weight than idiosyncratic experience.

Expertise and judgment become all the more critical in times of innovation. The Common Core State Standards represent a

potentially powerful opportunity or a disaster of titanic pro-
portions, depending on the decisional capital of the teaching
force and school leaders. Now that standards and assessments
are being spelled out, the difficulty will lie in how to develop the
best learning in relation to the standards. Some states may very
well provide specific directives that strip teachers of the opportunity to make independent judgments. Others may leave it to
the discretion of individual teachers, with equally problematic
results, unless they are part of a group that can draw on its own
professional capital.

I'll say more about CCSS in Chapter Six, but the point is that
more than ever, we will need the wisdom of decisional capital.
Education has entered the most volatile period in its history.
Schooling is not working for students or teachers or the public. The so-called 21st Century Skills, better called deep learning (critical thinking, creativity, and their ilk), seem crucial but
elusive. Technology has thrown a monkey wrench into the fray,
bringing with it giant potential and a mysterious downside. In
short, the decisional capital of teachers and the principals who
lead them will be at a premium in the circumstances we now face.

## Foster and Integrate

In their role of lead learner, principals are crucial to fostering
and integrating the three elements of professional capital. In
schools with strong professional capital, everyone knows that
the principal is immersed in improving instruction. Principals
do not directly lead many groups—teacher leaders do—but they
*participate*. They are in the group frequently, and their presence
is felt even when they are not there in person.

This strategy is economical. The more you as principal invest in human, social, and decisional capital, the less micro-energy and the fewer resources you need to squander on tedious, low-yield activity detached from the core of improvement, and the more help you get—lots of help—as teachers help each other. In essence, working within the professional capital framework leverages the resources of the group. Developing professional capital develops leadership across the school. This means that more gets done in the short run—because there are many leaders with a common focus—as sustainable leadership for the future is cultivated.

Two additional powerful forces arise from professional capital. I am going to call them *mutual allegiance* and *talk the walk*. When people work together, an inevitable human condition is evoked: they identify with and become committed to an entity larger than themselves. For example, when a principal undertakes the role of leading learning and begins to amass professional capital, the school moves from an individualistic culture to a collaborative one; teachers stop thinking about "their kids" only in "their classroom" and become committed to the success of all kids in the school. From there, when principals also work on professional capital in learning networks with other schools, they become almost as concerned about the success of other schools as they are about their own. Mutual allegiance is a powerful source of help, commiseration, and celebration for the collective good.

Greater professional capital and the collective success it engenders lead also to another surprising effect: school people learn to "talk the walk." I understand that you might confuse this phrase with "walk the talk" (meaning to honor one's word by one's deed). I call it talking the walk when people are doing something that is essential, deep, and related to success, and they are doing it using *common language* and *transparent actions*. We noticed this powerful by-product of our work in Ontario almost by accident. The discovery came when we organized unscripted visits to different schools and different districts. Individual teachers, principals, and indeed students were amazingly articulate, consistent, and specific in explaining what they were doing, why, and with what results. That's what I mean by being able to talk the walk.

The power of talking the walk cannot be overestimated. When individuals are required to explain themselves, they become clearer about what they are doing and why. When large numbers of individuals and groups can talk the walk, they become influential to each other and to others. There is only one way to gain this degree of shared understanding of the nature of the work, and that is by actually doing it with others day after day. That is the multiplicative power of professional capital.

## The More Powerful Way

It is crucial that the future of the principalship be centered around the more fundamental agenda of developing professional capital. The narrower alternative is that principals are channeled into functioning as instruments of the teacher effectiveness movement. They are given role descriptions and tools to micromanage and supervise teachers many times a year, and told that this is the main mechanism for improvement. If we continue down this path, it will be a bloody disaster. Learning does not work that way, for students or for adults. Checklists will never inspire teachers to give their heart and soul—or mind, for that matter.

Instead, the more powerful role of the principal consists of amassing and spending professional capital. He or she does that by seeking and then cultivating individual talent, including the development of new leaders. This is the acquiring and cherishing of human capital. The principal furthermore uses the group to change the group around the very specific agenda of strengthening social capital, whereby peers learn from each other in purposeful, specific ways to improve learning in the school. As this evolves, the principal seeks and reinforces the growing expertise of teachers to make expert decisions that dramatically improve learning for all students. This is decisional capital.

By way of reinforcing the line of argument I am pursuing, consider which of the following three strategies would have the most impact on improved decisional capital: performance appraisal, professional development, or collaborative cultures. Of course, I have loaded the deck. Performance appraisal can be useful (and should be incorporated in any organization) but is not intensive enough to "cause" deep learning. Similarly, professional development—workshops, even very good ones—will not be strong enough because it is what happens *in between workshops* that makes the difference. Hence we are back to collaborative cultures as the powerhouse because they embed all three components—day-to-day learning, performance appraisal, and integrated professional development. This is professional capital at its finest.

In the professional capital scenario, the principal does not lead all instructional learning. The principal does work to ensure that intense instructional focus and continuous learning are the core work of the school, and does this by being a talent scout and social engineer, building a culture for learning, tapping others to colead, and, well, basically being a learning leader for all.

We will return to the solution in Chapter Six, but more needs to be done to flesh out the new role of the principal. One aspect of the new role is that the principal will need to step outside the world of the school *in order to make the school better*.

One of the biases in a lot (not all) of the research on the principal is to treat the principal as if she or he ran the school as though it were an autonomous unit. In Chapter Four, we will correct that misconception by showing how ultimately the principal must operate as part and parcel of the larger system. Doing so is in his or her best interest, and benefits the system to boot. In any case, the maximizing principal knows that the heart of the organization is found in its core of professional capital, and for that core to flourish, the principal needs to be engaged in the outside as well as the inside of the school.

# Action Items

☐ As a principal, what do you orchestrate? Be specific.

☐ What are we doing to build professional capital?

☐ How would you characterize yourself right now in terms of Robinson's five leadership domains, especially number four (leading teacher learning and development)?

☐ How would you rate yourself or a principal you work with in terms of Bryk's combination of capacity, climate, community, and instruction?

☐ To what extent have you found yourself wasting time on teacher evaluation that has few useful consequences?

☐ How well does the professional capital concept work for you as a way to set priorities?

# Discuss with Colleagues

- Of the five main research efforts described in this chapter, which ones interest you most? Why?

- Compare notes on the question, "Who is my class?"

- What distinction needs to be made between "instructional leader" and "lead learner"?

·CHAPTER ONE·
Outmoded

·CHAPTER TWO·
Vices and Virtues

·CHAPTER THREE·
The First Key—Leading Learning

CHAPTER FOUR
The Second Key—Being a District
and System Player

·CHAPTER FIVE·
The Third Key—Becoming a
Change Agent

·CHAPTER SIX·
The Future Is Now

# The Second Key— Being a District and System Player

The boundary between the school and the outside is becoming more permeable. This has opened up an exciting new (and daunting) world for principals. Remember that the main goal is to use all resources, including those outside the school, to build the professional capital of teachers so that student learning can flourish. In so doing, principals need to become "system players"—school leaders who contribute to and benefit from the increased performance of other schools in the district and of the system as a whole. This new engagement of principals in the betterment of the system is in its early stages, so some aspects of it are not yet well developed.

By and large in this book, I have taken the perspective of the principal—what can he or she do to have greater impact on learning? In this chapter, I will necessarily refer to the role of the district (for example, how it can help develop the principalship), but it is not my intention to directly address the matter of how districts per se can improve.

If as a principal you go it alone, you can get only so far in developing a very good school. I would venture to say that although it is possible to become a great school despite the system you are in, it is not possible to *stay* effective if the system is not cultivating greatness in *all* of its schools.

I think it is this realization—that the system matters a great deal—that stimulated the Gates Foundation to shift its strategy to include school and district reform. Over the past four years, the foundation has invested heavily in the development of instruments to measure the performance of teachers in a program called MET (Measuring the Effectiveness of Teachers). Perhaps the Foundation realized, as I argued in

Chapter Two, that individual measures of feedback are insufficient drivers for system reform. Now it has launched a new initiative called iPD (innovative professional development) centered around the idea that whole districts can create a culture and practice of continuous learning for all of their teachers, and that districts can learn from each other. The principal is obviously a key factor in this mutual learning both within and across districts.

A system perspective makes sociological sense. If I am a good person in a bad society, I am not going to prosper as well as I might compared to moving to a better society or helping make the one I live in better. This is not as hard as it sounds when it comes to the current state of the principalship. Many jurisdictions are realizing that in the same way that you have to use the group to change the group within the school, they and you need to use the same approach when it comes to districtwide and statewide reform: you have to cultivate and leverage the savvy of the group—the schools in concert—in order to improve the system as a whole.

As for the individual principal who feels like a cog in a district or state machine, I will argue that it is in your own self-interest to be more proactive in relation to the larger system. And there are increasing opportunities to do so. In this chapter, I will identify some of these trends and invite you to exploit the possibilities.

## Looking Out to Improve Within

In Chapter Three, I quoted Lyle Kirtman (2013) and mentioned his having identified seven competencies of high-performing educational leaders. We will talk about all seven in the next chapter, but for now let's single out the seventh, which he calls *building external networks and partnerships*. This is the problem he found:

> Because the [current] consistent focus is on improving instruction by working internally, the time that leaders have for networking and building partnerships is decreasing. This internal focus is detrimental to strong leadership. The high-performing leaders build teams and delegate work and thereby find time to spend with parents, teachers, students, community members, school-system leaders, and other leaders inside and outside of education. These networks produce new ideas, practices, and materials that can be effectively used *to improve results in their own schools*. (Kirtman, 2013, p. 8, emphasis added)

The point is not for you as principal to pay less attention to intraschool matters but rather to engage outside *in order to increase learning within your school* (while at the same time contributing to the betterment of the system). Engage externally in order to buttress your work of building internal capacity (human, social, and decisional capital). Align internal and external forces. Be selfish: as part of a cluster of schools, you can use that network to improve your own school by accessing new ideas, and by participating in networks, you create another source of pressure accompanied by ideas for you and your staff to take action. Be selfless, too: most humans get satisfaction from contributing to the wider good. Have your cake and eat it, too. But don't just take my word for it. Be self-conscious about whether what you are doing is working. Question whether what you get from outside is proving useful in your school, and challenge yourself by seeking evidence as to whether or not what you are doing is working as well as learning from what's done elsewhere.

There are at least two faces of the outside: intradistrict development, and learning beyond the district.

# Intradistrict Development

Even if you are in a district that is not promoting the notion that schools can learn from each other, you will be better off if you help your staff connect to one or more other schools in the district; all the better if you are in a district that does promote such exchange.

## School to School

Let's look at three intradistrict, school-to-school examples: Park Manor, and two other schools we recently filmed in Ontario; Sanger Unified School District in California, and the Communities of Practice (COP) schools in Edmonton, Alberta.

Park Manor, which we discussed in Chapter Three, is a senior public school (grades 6–8) in Elmira, Ontario, in the Waterloo Region District School Board. We've already seen that its principal, James Bond, is proactive and supportive of developing the professional capital of teachers within the school. Linking to the outside is a natural extension of the journey. As lead teacher Liz Anderson informed us, Bond increasingly enables teachers to showcase the work of the school to outsiders, connect the school with other resources (such as researchers and the Ministry of Education), present at conferences, and become part of wider networks.

We see similar activities at the other two schools we filmed in another Ontario district—William G. Davis Sr. Public School and Central Peel Secondary School—based in the Peel District School Board just outside Toronto. As these two schools progress, the principals—Andreas Meyer at W. G. Davis, and Lawrence De Maeyer at Central Peel—expect their teachers to participate and participate themselves in learning exchanges with other schools in the district (and beyond, as I'll describe later). What is happening in Peel, for example, is that principals as peers have started to build rapport and mutual commitments. It is interesting to note that the principals have been pushing the district to move in this direction as much as the other way round. Principals, in short, use connection with peers within the district and their new relationships to contribute to changing the culture of the district. At the same time, district leadership, in Peel at least, welcome these bottom-up energies and indeed formulated policies and strategies to leverage them (such as passing a BYOD policy and allocating funds so that all 246 schools now have wireless access capacity).

Our California example is the Sanger district, where we filmed in 2010. In this case, the district was the initiator of school-to-school learning, and here my point is that principals need to take advantage when such an opportunity appears. Sanger is a small (twenty schools), high-poverty district in Fresno. I look here at only one aspect of its strategy. Every school is in a cluster with three or four other schools. Leadership teams from each school meet four times a year (hosted by each school in turn) with a specific agenda (how to improve math, best approaches for English Language Learners, and so on).

Cross-visits of subsets of teachers are arranged to share practices that are getting results. Each June, the cluster convenes a "summit" during which each school in turn presents to the other three and to district leaders their progress over the year: what they had set out to accomplish, strategies used, results obtained, lessons learned, key questions, and so on. Principals learn to take full advantage of the networks to stimulate their own school development and to contribute to that of others.

The good work in Sanger has recently been verified by Jane David and Joan Talbert (2013), two scholars who have worked for decades researching school and district improvement. They found that Sanger built its success on three principles: "change is developmental," decisions are "grounded in evidence," and there is an "emphasis on relationships and respect" for adults as well as for students (p. 8)—all ideas compatible with what I have been presenting.

Our third example, the Edmonton Public Schools' COP, provides a variation along the same lines (Edmonton Public Schools, 2013). Edmonton is a large district within which some principals and teachers get together, with some support from the district, to use technology to learn collaboratively while increasing the use of technology per se in learning within their schools. The COP has two components:

1. **A persistent online community site** where staff could share reflections, find information, and ask questions of their colleagues

2. **Regular face-to-face sessions** that emphasize sharing between teachers and plenty of time to explore and collaborate

School principals facilitate this work among their teachers and also use it for their own development. As reported by one member of a principal network focused on developing and leading professional learning communities, which is one of the activities within the COP:

> One of the goals of this team is to increase the leadership capacity of its members through participation in regular professional development. Our efforts have produced an archive of invaluable resources that principals frequently access to advance the work of their individual schools. (Personal communication, May 2013)

, , ,

In these three examples, you don't see schools working in isolation. Principals and teachers from different schools learn from each other. Schools get stronger because the district and other schools are getting stronger.

## District Coherence

The examples I just outlined are not focused on the district per se. Those efforts are mainly happening school to school. The learning is more lateral—across schools—than it is hierarchical. But it may be helpful here to look at the work from the perspective of how complex systems can *cohere*. In Figure 4.1, I attempt to capture the overall picture of districtwide coherence. Top-down structural alignment—coordinating formal polices and the like—does not create coherence in itself, because coherence requires greater unity of mind-set—a shared mind-set, really.

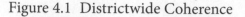

Figure 4.1  Districtwide Coherence

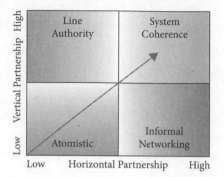

Large-scale success will occur only when system members begin to act from a shared, coherent mind-set. The only way to develop a shared mind-set is through purposeful and continuous interaction and learning over a period of time.

In any system, coherence is a function of the combination of vertical and horizontal rapport. The glue of coherence is purposeful interaction over time that people find worthwhile— for example, in terms of results. In the figure, the vertical axis denotes the degree of partnership between schools on the one hand, the district on the other. The horizontal denotes the extent of interaction among peer principals.

Let's start with the least desirable quadrants. The low-low quadrant—bottom left—represents the traditional loosely coupled operation. As some have observed, this can be characterized as a system of individual schools, not a school system. I have called it atomistic: schools operate on their own; some do well, but most don't. In the bottom-right quadrant, probably the least frequently found these days, the district provides little direction, and schools band together informally for political and technical support, and maybe even as a counterforce when the district imposes new requirements that principals do not value.

The top two quadrants interest us more. All successful districts develop strong two-way relationships with their schools. For the past two decades, my colleague Ken Leithwood (2011) has studied in detail the characteristics and performance of high-performing districts. He has found that such districts develop four key capacities:

1. **Core processes** (widely shared goals, instructional expertise, data, and evidence)
2. **Supporting conditions** (implementation plans, professional development, alignment of policies)
3. **Relationships** (collaboration within and outside the district)
4. **Leadership** (at the district and school levels)

Districts that have a strong relationship between the center and the schools (the top left quadrant in Figure 4.1) can yield strong results in the short run. There will be a focused agenda, tight capacity building, close monitoring of results, and often a propensity to replace principals sooner than later if they don't measure up. Principals become deeply committed to their own school in the context of what the district is attempting to accomplish. The system self-selects instructionally focused principals. These systems can be very good for improving student achievement—again, in the short run—but they can also be vulnerable to the too-narrow tendencies we discussed in Chapter Two. In other words, strong line authority is not the solution, even though it can yield some results. In effect, I am suggesting that principals seek lateral relationships as much as vertical ones.

For you as a principal, the bottom line is to build the professional capital of your teachers, drawing on their mutual learning, enhanced by learning from other schools. A key goal for you, then (and one that would also benefit districts), is to seek to learn from other schools, zero in on practices that help your own school, and in so doing also achieve a degree of consistency across schools (as good practices get retained). You learn from other schools at the same time that you have strong two-way learning relationships with the district. Indeed, district leaders who want overall coherence realize that it is in their best interests to foster school-to-school learning. These systems achieve coherence because they foster both vertical and lateral interaction (top right-hand quadrant).

Currently, districts commonly neglect this strategy of actively developing and supporting purposeful peer learning across schools. In their big study of leadership and student achievement, Leithwood and Seashore Louis (2012) found that almost 60 percent of principals surveyed indicated that their districts only occasionally provided them with opportunities to work productively with colleagues from other schools. I am reminded of the old joke about leadership: keep the half of your followers who hate your guts from talking to the other half, who haven't yet made up their minds.

In any case, effective leaders who have their vertical act together, whether they are superintendents or principals, also invest in peer learning strategies. They deliberately loosen their "authority grip" in order to gain indirectly a better "system grip" (coherence) through the interaction of the group. When principals and schools work together under the guidance of the system, the whole system improves, in the same way that the whole school improves when teachers collaborate under the guidance of the principal.

# Beyond the District

These days, with access to the world made easier by technology, schools should also look to schools outside their boundaries. If you are starting something new and there is little direct expertise in the district on the topic, if you are in very small district with few schools to draw on, or if you really want to explore what might be new by connecting to external sources of innovation, you need to see the world as your arena of ideas. I look at three examples here.

## Peel District, Ontario

When Peel District in Ontario decided it could no longer run its system of 246 schools from the center, it encouraged the schools to explore the world more widely. Several school principals and district leaders conducted site visits to external jurisdictions that were using technology to further pedagogy. This ignited the spark that led to those and other schools taking off in new directions. As I have mentioned, we filmed two of the Peel schools, and can attest that the ideas spread like wildfire; the principal and teacher leadership teams in each school built their own version quite rapidly (within two years). *Every* classroom in the two schools (one with 350 students and one with 935) is a hive of engagement, each an amazing example of positive contagion of new ideas. It is too early to tell if these new developments will translate into improved student achievement, although this certainly was the case at Park Manor (discussed in Chapter Three).

In these cases, external catalysts and internal combustion combined to generate change with seemingly little overt effort (more about this organic, positive contagion change phenom-enon in Chapter Six). What is particularly pertinent to the professional capital agenda is that the principals and teachers learned together. It is true that principals networking among themselves would be useful, but their participating as learners alongside their teachers is much more powerful.

Learning externally is all the better when the district fosters such engagement, as shown in the next two examples—one on a small scale, and the other much more ambitious.

### School District 96, Illinois

District 96 in Illinois has fewer than fifteen schools. The super-intendent, Tom Many, and school leaders built up a strong PLC within and across the schools during the first decade of this century. They were quite successful in terms of impact on student achievement across the system, but they wanted ideas from beyond their own borders. Drawing on the concept of schools learning from other schools (which I have called "lat-eral capacity building"), Tom came up with the idea that each school should link up with a "sister school" in the region but outside the district. The idea was that each would find a school with similar interests and goals, and the pair would work on them together. The district facilitated this process. Some prin-cipals were skeptical about its value but were willing to try it. After the process was under way for a year, I asked Tom to send me a note about how the strategy was faring. Here is his reply:

> The sister school exchange began with a small pilot three years ago and has grown a bit larger each year. We are tapping into lateral capacity through the lens of professional learning

communities, and reinforcing the learning with an end-of-the-year learning fair. The results of this project have been very powerful.

Planning and participating in a sister school exchange is now a required professional development activity for each building principal and has been incorporated into his or her school improvement planning effort.

Each principal is required to identify a sister school that has a reputation for expertise in a specific area related to the principal's school improvement plan. The expectation is that the area of excellence or expertise that the sister school possesses is connected and associated with the principal's school improvement goals for that year. In its simplest form, principals are asked to reach out through their networks and find a school that has demonstrated they are successfully dealing with an area of need for the principal's own school.

We have discovered that the learning is two-way. Obviously, we learn a lot from the schools we visit, the program we observe, and the teachers with whom we talk. The best way for people to change is to do it themselves, and to learn from others similarly engaged. To see other people who are a lot like them being successful with the change is powerful and specific. Watching other people who are a lot like you generates so many positive results. We found that if the principal targets his or her sister school visit carefully, the visit can do more to help his or her teachers learn and grow than any "sit and get" in-service program.

We have found the reverse is also true as well. We learn from others when we visit their school, but when the sister schools come to visit District 96, our teachers learn as they prepare to present information about our practices to the other school. Anytime our teachers have to prepare and present, they report that they learn at a deeper level. Teachers report that the process of preparing to speak to visitors is very powerful in terms of sustaining our practices and driving them deeper into our culture.

I have not heard a single negative comment about the sister school exchange idea, and in most cases the teachers who have participated are not only positive but rave about what they learned and how successful the experience was in helping them see other ways to improve their teaching and learning. If this is lateral capacity, then we need more of it! (Tom Many, personal communication, July 2009, adapted from Fullan, 2011c)

Clearly this is a small, informal, high-yield (low-cost, high-payoff) strategy that would be especially valuable for small rural school districts. Exchanges beyond one's own district do not have to be fancy, but they should be purposeful, specific, and linked to a learning goal and evidence of impact. My guess is that once these principals experience the value of this strategy, they will be inclined to do more of it on their own.

## California

California presents an interesting case for whole-system change. It is large and complex—larger in population than all of Canada (thirty-eight versus thirty-five million), with seven million students and over one thousand school districts. Both the governor and the state superintendent of public instruction are elected. California was a leading innovative state in the 1960s, but has been in steady decline since. Beneath the surface of continuous failure have been pockets of success (such as Sanger), and an unfulfilled desire on the part of many educators to turn the tide. There are now a favorable set of conditions that could in fact fundamentally alter the future:

a governor, Jerry Brown, who favors local development and reform; a superintendent, Tom Torlakson, who wants the state department of education to shift to a focus on capacity building over compliance; district superintendents, individually and as an association, to work on improvement including networks; a union, the California Teachers Association, that favors the professional capital agenda; and, for the first time in thirty years, *money*. It is beyond the scope of this book to address the matter of state reform, but we can see emerging a strategy that engages schools and districts as system players learning from each other.

One of the early manifestations of this new way is a group called California Office for Reform in Education (http://core districts.org). I offer one caution as I introduce this example. CORE is still at its early stage, and several important issues have to be worked out in the relationships with the union, the state department of education, and the federal government. Stay tuned, as they say. For our purposes, it serves as an example of how schools and districts can work with, learn from, and improve themselves.

The CORE group was originally formed to pursue a Race to the Top grant. When its bid was unsuccessful, the group decided to continue anyway. CORE has its own CEO and secretariat and currently consists of ten districts that serve over one million students.

Here is its mission statement (California Office to Reform Education, 2012):

"As a collaboration of districts, we work together to innovate, implement, and scale new strategies and tools that help our students succeed, so that our districts are improved to meet the challenges of the 21st Century."

CORE has formulated "design principles" (instruction focused, practice oriented, and unwaveringly committed to equity), and strives to be data driven, outcomes focused, educator driven, and clear and accessible in terms of what it shares. The group recently applied to the California State Board of Education, and the federal government for a waiver from certain NCLB requirements, not to gain freedom from accountability but rather, in their words, to enhance it. Here is wording from its waiver request (California Office to Reform Education, 2012):

> CORE's waiver is rooted in shared learning and responsibility for student achievement. It is designed to instill a new collective and individual moral imperative to prepare all students for successful futures—nested in the specific needs of California students, with an all-encompassing focus on eliminating disparities between subgroups. This plan is grounded in the concept of moral imperative.
>
> With this waiver, CORE does not seek to escape from accountability. Instead, CORE is asking for a waiver to a new system with a higher level of shared responsibility and accountability but built on the right drivers to improve our system: *all* students prepared for college and careers, and the elimination of disparity and disproportionality on multiple critical measures of student success.
>
> In short, this waiver will allow us to establish a demonstrated system of accountability within and across participating districts that will meet and exceed state and Federal forms of accountability. In so doing it will result in documented improvements in student learning and achievement.

Further it will incorporate other districts in a growing network of high-performing districts.

In an unprecedented action (giving waivers to districts), Arne Duncan, federal secretary of education, approved the waiver for one year in August 2013. Again I leave the politics aside. (Among other things CORE is still stuck with the wrong accountability requirements relative to teacher accountability, which I have discussed in Chapter Three.)

On the strategy front, one of the very first actions that CORE is taking is to establish a strategy whereby successful schools can help less successful schools with similar demographics. CORE's assumption is that the helper will gain as much from the exchange as the "helpee." The strategy uses all the "right drivers" we discussed in Chapter Two: capacity building, social capital, pedagogy, and systemness (although it is trying to finesse the individual teacher accountability requirements within the context of the right drivers). CORE will develop guidelines for the partnerships, training and support materials for capacity building, and indicators of success. This is an attempt to develop professional capital on a large scale by developing and using the resources of the districts themselves as well as outside expertise.

Sticking with the principal, the point is that district collaboratives present new opportunities for principals to learn from each other on a much wider scale for the benefit of their own schools and districts. In so doing, they can become better change leaders. If you will allow me to put on my system hat for a moment, a bigger question is, how can an exceedingly complex and large system (in this case, a state that is the ninth-largest economy in the world) achieve a degree of coherence of the kind we are

talking about in this chapter? On this matter of the whole system, the California legislature passed a new piece of legislation
in September 2013 to establish a new entity called the California
Collaborative for Education Excellence (CCEE). The language of
the legislation is couched in terms of partnerships with local districts and networks, and a "programmatic peer support model
that drives capacity for continuous improvement at the local
level." There can be many a slip twixt the cup and the lip, so it
remains to be seen how CCEE will work in relation to one thousand districts, but it is clearly in the direction of the ideas in this
chapter. Even if CCEE does not pan out, various groups we are
working with in California are committed to promoting and
funding clusters of school districts working together on the
agenda multi-school and district improvement.

I call this strategy "leadership from the middle" (that is, districts), following what Andy Hargreaves and Henry Braun (also
at Boston College) (2012) found when they studied ten districts
in Ontario that worked together to improve special education
inclusion. If a top-down approach can't work in a big, complex
system, and if bottom-up approaches are always desultory, the
idea is to get some of the glue and energy from people in the
middle who will work laterally with other districts, and partner
with agencies at the state level in a common pursuit of raising
the bar and closing the gap for all students. If the middle starts
to cohere, it will become a better partner for other elements of
the system. If there ever was a win-win proposition under conditions of complexity, this is it! Success won't be easy, but one
can readily envisage the strategy.

, , ,

Structured approaches like those used in District 96 and CORE aside, there are many informal opportunities for principals to build external networks that will benefit their schools and districts. Even within districts that do not have strong internal coherence, principals can collaborate informally with other schools and thereby become a force for district coherence. My point is that principals and the people who govern them should promote this wider learning within and across districts, as long as it is coupled with the internal focus that we discussed in Chapter Three.

## Not You Alone

This chapter has argued that we have failed to use the lateral resources in the system to leverage greater success. The point is brought home forcefully in *Unseen Children*, a recent report by the Office for Standards in Education (2013) that examines progress over the past twenty years in the seven most deprived areas in England. The report concluded that the schools that did not improve experienced several forms of "disconnection." One type involved poor relationships within the school and with local communities; another disconnection pertained to the schools' isolation from other schools. These disconnected schools "had insufficient contact with other successful schools." In other words, the persistently unsuccessful schools had never seen a successful school with the same demographics as their own (even though these schools existed). The unsuccessful schools "worked alone and didn't benefit from the sharing of new and innovative practices" (p. 9). These schools did not access the professional capital that was perhaps only a few miles away. They stayed isolated, and they have stayed stuck for the past twenty years—unseen children indeed.

In sum, to maximize impact, the principal must seek ideas from other similar schools that perhaps have had more success, and must see herself or himself as a system player. When the ideas of thousands of principals are unleashed and shared, imagine the resources. When principals form productive partnerships with other schools, consider the support they can gain through regular interaction between their staff and that of other schools.

The fact is, most effective leaders want to make a contribution beyond their own borders. I have met scores of such leaders, and they are not megalomaniacs but in fact the opposite. They are humble. But they want to learn more, and they want to think that they have something to offer that will benefit others. They don't want money or glory, but they do want a bigger platform from which to maximize their impact. They make perfect change agents, because they push upward and laterally from the bottom and the middle. So, what are the core competencies of change agents? Chapter Five takes up this crucial matter.

# Action Items

☐ What boundaries have you been slow to cross? Why?

☐ Whom in your district have you put off getting to know? What can you do about that?

☐ What school-to-school bonds could you explore, based on common interests?

☐ Are there schools like yours that have had more success?

☐ What could you be more proactive about in relation to the district or other systems that affect your work as principal?

# Discuss with Colleagues

- How coherent is your district? If its coherence is less than perfect, what holds things back?

- What are colleagues doing that you might also do to be more active and visible in your district or larger system?

- What issue(s) would we like to discuss with district-level people? How can we get that started?

- What could we as an administration team be doing to boost the principal's role in the system?

# CHAPTER · FIVE

# The Third Key—
# Becoming a Change
# Agent

**P**rincipal, this chapter is about your qualities as a leader of change. How good are you at moving people and organizations forward under very difficult circumstances? The goal of this chapter is to make you and the vast majority of your colleagues truly the second-most important players in the education of students.

In his classic advice book for Renaissance leaders, *The Prince*, Niccolo Machiavelli counseled them about the challenges involved in establishing a new order of things. He said that those who are against the change will be vociferous and aggressive, while those potentially in favor will be timid and lukewarm in their support. The reason is that the opposers know concretely what they will be losing. The loss is immediate, palpable, and emotional. Those potentially in favor know only *theoretically* what the change might bring. The benefits are in the distance, abstract, and unknown. It is less that the would-be supporters are cowards and more that they are unclear and lack confidence because they cannot envisage the outcome.

In my view, in modern times the leader's role is to work through and help others work through these ambiguities—sometimes by overcoming resistance, but mostly by reassuring the potential losers that there is something to gain; other times by helping the willing gain the grounded confidence that is essential to success. Ambiguity does not release a leader from the need to take action. The business professor and consultant team of Jeffrey Pfeffer and Robert Sutton (2006) captured this well in their definition of wisdom: "the ability to act with knowledge while doubting what you know" (p. 174). A change agent embodies this kind of wisdom—acting sooner than later but always alert to feedback.

# Change Agency

We can derive additional excellent guidance for principals through discussion of recent examinations of leaders as they work to find their way (and the way of those with whom they work) in change. In the following sections, I consider two sources that are mutually consistent and insightful relative to the theme of maximizing impact and at the same time improving at leading for change. One source is Cal Newport, a Georgetown computer science professor given to supplying students with unconventional advice; the other is Lyle Kirtman. As we look at their orientations, allow me also to use them as a framework for further thoughts of my own about the principal's role as key agent of change.

## Mastery and Passion: A Mutual Feed

Newport's book (2012) is called *So Good They Can't Ignore You*. I like how it starts off with the jarring statement, "'Follow your passion' is dangerous advice." This is not as incompatible as it seems with my own strong advice that education reform is about the "moral imperative realized" (2011c). The moral imperative concerns the deep belief that leaders must lead the organization in "raising the bar and closing the gap" of learning for *all* students, regardless of background. I include "realized" in the phrase to suggest that the only measure that counts is the one which shows that you are actually getting somewhere on this agenda to enable all to be successful. This seems straightforward until we find that some leaders can have *too much moral imperative* (or at least be too morally *imperious*) when they are

not clear about how to realize it, browbeat people without helping them, or speak a passionate rhetoric that is not as deep as
it appears. All of this is to say that passion matters but must be
*earned* through actually getting better at leading change—the
latter achieved through a process of learning that does depend
to some degree on trial and error. I would go so far as to say
that you only really feel the passion emotionally when you
are skilled at the work and are actually experiencing success.
Passion without skill is dangerous.

On the one hand, yes, if you happen to have it, pursue your
fervent passion into effective action; but don't feel bad if you
start without great fire in your belly. Fan the cinders of action,
and you will discover and amplify your passion through experience. When I was thirty, even forty, I had little passion about
education change. It was an intellectual interest. As I got better
at it over more than a decade, I became more and more passionately engaged in wanting to work with others to solve vexing
change problems that brought benefit to others and to me. This
is Cal Newport's message for many of us, "skills trump passion
in the quest for work you love" (2012) For me, caring to learn
was the route to learning to care.

On the other hand, if your passion is already rich, park it
for a bit while you focus on your *abilities as change agent*. As
Newport says, "Don't follow your passion; rather, let it follow
*you* in your quest to become, in the words of . . . Steve Martin . . . ,
'so good they can't ignore you'" (2012, p. xx). Passion, according
to Newport, is often a side effect of mastery. Mastery and passion feed on each other. The ten-thousand-hour rule—getting
better and better at something through deliberate skill development and practice—is basically about the perfection of craft.

But in a real sense, the more you learn for yourself and the more skilled you become, the more passionate you will also become about the quality and value of your work.

One necessity for improvement—poorly developed in education, as we have seen—is receiving constructive feedback on an ongoing basis. If you focus on skill (and we will shortly identify very specific leadership qualities), you can readily see that becoming more effective is the main point. By contrast, it is hard to imagine that getting direct feedback on your degree of *passion*—advice that you have it or that you don't, or encouragement to increase it—is going to be very helpful, although it probably will not do much harm. In my own case, as I have said, my passion for my work increased as my expertise increased. It is difficult to be deeply passionate about something if you are not getting better at it. I (think) I love golf, but I would love it more if I were any good at it.

In Chapter Three, I introduced the three elements of professional capital that a leader in learning helps the organization amass. Newport adds another type of capital that is more personal to your occupation. He uses the concept of "career capital" to define the skills and abilities you have developed. He says that there is nothing wrong with trying a job you might not be sure of as long it allows you to develop particular new skills. The more skills you develop, the more choices you will have and the more likely you will be to recognize work that kindles your passion. Newport introduces the idea of mission, basically arguing that developing your career capital (skills and abilities) will likely lead to a sense of mission, defined as the desire to make a difference in an area that has meaning for you and *that you are good at.*

My own, complementary conclusion is that you will never end up being satisfied, let alone effective, if you are doing something that you are not good at. The ever-passionate superintendent who moves from job to job may appear to be having a successful career—but my guess is that such people are not very happy and that their reputations catch up with them. In any case, such people do not make effective leaders, as their flames burn only too briefly.

The message for you as a principal who wants to maximize your power to change your school is to focus on developing and mastering your skills relative to the agenda described in Chapters Three and Four. In doing so, you will end up passionately loving what you do. Also think about the leaders of change over the years whom you admire, whether they are historical figures or the principal at the next school over. If you look closely, you are likely to find highly skilled individuals whose passion as much reflects their effectiveness as the reverse.

## Skills for Leading Change

Several times earlier in this book, I cited Lyle Kirtman (2013) and promised to address his overall set of seven leadership competencies. The core characteristics for effective leaders that he identifies in *Leadership and Teams: The Missing Piece of the Education Reform Puzzle* are entirely congruent with the themes of this book, and I find them helpful for our purposes because they are in the form of specific competencies. As you think about the change agenda that I laid out in Chapters Three and Four, use Kirtman's set of skills as a template for your own development as a leader. You will find that strengthening these seven competencies will help you develop professional capital inside and outside your school. Building these seven competencies will automatically feed into the work of developing professional capital, and vice versa. According to Kirtman, a competent leader:

1. Challenges the status quo.
2. Builds trust through clear communications and expectations.
3. Creates a commonly owned plan for success.
4. Focuses on team over self.
5. Has a sense of urgency for sustainable results.
6. Commits to continuous improvement for self.
7. Builds external networks and partnerships.

Before looking at some of the elements within each of the seven, we can immediately observe two fundamental issues in regard to the set. First, it is unlikely that a leader is going to master these competencies by confining his or her leadership by trying to directly improve teachers' classroom instruction. Rather, an effective leader spends time on—gets better at—all seven domains and their interconnections in order that *the whole organization* generates measurable instructional improvement.

Second, there are orientations and skills in the set that will take a very long while to master. If you are a young leader, get going on this personal learning agenda: develop your career capital. If you are a more seasoned leader, examine which competencies you are good at and which ones might represent weaknesses, and learn accordingly. In either case, you will want to complete the leadership assessment inventory that Kirtman uses in his work with schools. The inventory contains thirty-five subitems across the seven competencies (Kirtman, 2013, pp. 193–208). When you get inside the seven competencies, you find items familiar to what we have covered so far in this book.

The point about all these competencies is that you need to assess your own profile, appreciate and reinforce your strengths, and address those areas that are less well developed. Kirtman's book is one place to go, but so are professional development courses that feature closely similar components. Perhaps the best way is to learn from leaders who model these competencies and to practice them yourself with feedback from others. When you develop new skills in a given area, you also become more clear about it because skills reveal how a given phenomenon works. In short, skill development creates clarity and fans passion. Here are the seven competencies.

### 1. Challenge the Status Quo

Challenging the status quo includes the willingness and ability to question common practices, take risks, explore innovations, and not let rules slow down action. These leaders have an eye on the end game, which in our case is improving the learning of all students. They tend to challenge current practices that are not likely to increase student achievement. They are willing to take risks to achieve results, and are more interested in motivating people than in following narrow rules. As they develop the skill set—the seven competencies—they are in a better position to challenge the status quo effectively because they create the conditions for overall success. You might say that such a leader doesn't mind rocking the boat (at the beginning of the change process) because he or she has the other six competencies to rely on.

## 2. Build Trust Through Clear Communications and Expectations

I like to adapt one of Stephen Covey's insights, "You can't talk your way out of what you've behaved yourself into" (2004), by saying that you can't talk your way into trust. I mean that you can only "behave" your way into it by naming, modeling, and monitoring your trustworthiness. You name trust as a value and norm that you will embrace and develop in the organization; you model it in your day-to-day actions; and you monitor it in your own and others' behavior.

Note that trustworthiness goes beyond integrity to include real competence as well. You have to be true to your word, but also very good at what you do. According to Kirtman, spreading trust also entails mastering directness and honesty about performance expectations; following through with actions on commitments made; ensuring clear understanding of key communications; and being comfortable in dealing with conflict.

## 3. Create a Commonly Owned Plan for Success

In this third skill set, Kirtman confirms what many of us have found about implementation plans: far too many of them remain only on paper. Time and again, we have seen implementation plans that look great visually but are too complex or general to give any guidance in action. As I advised in *Motion Leadership* (2010b), "beware of fat plans." When plans are elaborate, they rarely are clear enough to be understood and actionable. When plans focus on a few clear goals and corresponding actions, they are much more likely to stimulate action.

Kirtman highlights working on buy-in or ownership of the plan; monitoring how well it works, making corresponding adjustments and engaging in regular two-way communication; and having clear measurement for each key goal in the plan. Plans on paper might look great, but they mean nothing unless they come alive through practice. It's important to remember that implementation plans are not for the planners; they are for the implementers. Thus, as I concluded in *Motion Leadership* and as Kirtman implies, plans have to be "sticky"—concise, actionable, memorable, tied closely to action—thereby becoming internalized by all.

At the beginning, it is less important that the plan meet everyone's approval than that the plan starts a process of buy-in. The starting aim of the plan should be to focus a leadership team on the task of building capacity for success. The development of professional capital as described in Chapter Three is essentially a process for creating skilled, shared ownership. Furthermore, because engagement of all organization members is required for success, the plan should be systemic in the sense that it affects everyone. Monitoring should concentrate on keeping track of whether actions yield engagement and results. Every plan should be alterable, as ongoing needs require. Although approval doesn't need to be universal at the start, if the plan is really working, it should steadily become internalized among those who take part in its implementation.

## 4. Focus on Team over Self

Change-agent principals who focus on team over self hire the best people for the team (invest in human capital), build a team environment (social capital), support the learning of all staff, and seek critical feedback. They hire people who don't simply take orders (or worse, passively ignore directives). They foster group norms such that people feel free to raise concerns and offer alternative ideas. As the principal focuses the talk on solving a problem instead of on complaints and scapegoating, the school builds trust among its working members. They come to trust the process because it proves itself more times than not. As Kirtman says, "These leaders hire the best and never settle for less" (p. 7). The quality of the team uplifts everyone.

## 5. Have a Sense of Urgency for Sustainable Results

In Chapter Two, I said that although not all urgency is productive, a high sense of urgency does matter and needs to be targeted in a manner that mobilizes people to tackle core issues. As we saw earlier, Cal Newport observed that passion itself does not necessarily lead to results and becomes a problem in the absence of skill. Passion *without skill*, he said, is useless if not dangerous. The message for leaders is to build professional capital as part and parcel of passion and urgency.

In the context of his seven domains of competence, it makes sense to me that Kirtman placed urgency as number 5, because the preceding four domains make organizations and their leaders more skillful, enabling them to push effectively for greater urgency. As those skills become stronger, Kirtman's leaders have no compunction against demanding action and results. By building their own skills and those of others, they earn enough leadership capital (which in effect is decisional capital for leaders) to "get away with" decisive action. They get away with it because they have proven themselves to be trustworthy *and* competent. As Kirtman found, they are anxious to move initiatives ahead and can be very decisive, use data to support their actions, and reinforce a clear systemic direction for the organization. They want results, but results that are authentic. The previous four competencies help develop the skills and motivation required for the group to be effective at getting results that can be sustained. Within this group action, members appreciate it when leaders "take charge" expressing and acting on a sence of urgency.

### 6. Commit to Continuous Improvement for Self

Effective change agents have steadfast purpose, but they are alert to evidence. When the *Economist* recently reported on personality tests for managers, they highlighted one aspect of a Korn/Ferry test: that what good leaders have in common is "a willingness to let new evidence change their views" ("Emotional Breakdown," 2013). I suspect that leaders with deep passion are sometimes blinded by their fervor and thus do not remain alert to evidence that could cause them to rethink how they might approach a given situation more effectively.

Think of "continuous improvement for self" as your ever-present backup plan. If you are going to be decisive, you had better be always learning. Kirtman notes that in being committed to continuous improvement for self, outstanding leaders wonder how to get better results, seek innovative ideas from all team members, take responsibility for their mistakes, and are in general preoccupied with learning to become better and helping team members do so as well.

### 7. Build External Networks and Partnerships

In Chapter Four, I discussed this seventh competency, building external networks and partnerships. Keeping the individual school focused, changing, yet still in running order is one priority; but change-agent principals know several reasons for also staying dynamically plugged in to the external world: they get new ideas; doing so keeps the pressure on; and along the way, they often need outside partners for political and technical reasons. When you have partners, such as districts that are different, you are more likely to encounter new ideas—what Steven Johnson (2010) called getting ideas from "the adjacent possible," a term he borrowed from chaos theory.

Moreover, it is not a bad idea to contribute to the betterment of the bigger picture. To make a contribution beyond your own bailiwick is a basic human virtue. Selfishly speaking, if you don't help improve the system, your neglect will come back to haunt you, or your grandchildren.

, , ,

The seven competencies are aimed at building your capacity at both the personal and the organizational level, and they imply that you need to comprehend how your leadership style can both enhance and hinder capacity building in the school. Principals must understand how their leadership team, their teachers, and the culture of the school all have an impact on building professional capital. The current narrow emphasis on instructional leadership that I've described throughout this book has negated the necessary more complete focus on management, group development, and implementation. Leadership, in short, includes instruction but is much more than that. If leaders neglect management and their other crucial roles, instruction will suffer as well.

# Distorted Mirrors

In my book *Change Leader* (2011b), I cited a leadership qual-ity called "know thy impact" which I derived from research that has shown that leaders (all of us really) tend to have a dis-torted, often more favorable image of how we come across to those who work with us. We are often oblivious to this phe-nomenon. Research continues to corroborate this finding. In a series of experiments, Sebastien Brion of the Business School at the University of Navarra (Spain) and Cameron Anderson of the Haas School of Business at UC Berkeley found that leaders often overestimated "how much others in the organization were allied to them" (Brion & Anderson, 2013, p. 129). They call this the "illusion of alliance." Because of this blind spot, these lead-ers failed to nurture and maintain the relationships that would have been necessary for success. The message is, don't take rela-tionships for granted. The engaged principal is always building and tending to relationships. Because they build strong teams, encourage feedback, and alternative viewpoints, and because they participate as learners, they are in fact more likely to pick up cues that certain relationships require attention.

There are other distortions that the reflective principal will need to be alert to. Robert Kaplan and Robert Kaiser, two busi-ness consultants who specialize in selecting and improving leaders, fittingly titled their book *Fear Your Strengths: What You Are Best at Could Be Your Biggest Problem* (2013). Their con-clusions are entirely compatible with the themes in this book. Let's just take one continuum that Kaplan and Kaiser discuss—being passionately *forceful* versus being *enabling*—and see how each extreme can backfire. The forceful, passionate leader can "stake out positions too early," shutting down the introvert or otherwise leading people to agree too readily with the leader without bringing their best ideas into the situation (p. 8). Or such leaders can become abusive and preemptory in the face of disagreement. If someone combines passion with intellect, you could have the overly articulate dominator who always has something impressive to say. I am reminded of the story of an exchange between jazz musician John Coltrane and composer, musician, and bandleader Miles Davis. Coltrane had the habit of playing too long once he was on a roll. One time when Davis complained to him that it was interfering with the flow of the group, Coltrane said, "I can't stop playing," to which Davis replied, "Try taking the horn out of your mouth." Some leaders, as impressive as they may sound, don't know when to take the horn out of their mouth.

By being less forceful and more enabling, you can also overdo it. Committed to trusting, listening, and consulting with everyone, such leaders, according to Kaplan and Kaiser, can be too indecisive; they may trust without verifying, be "too nice," and generally be prone to automatic collaboration amounting to dithering.

Too forceful, not forceful enough: welcome to the world of leadership where *judgment* is the coin of decisional capital. The most basic piece of advice is to work on your own weakness. If you are an overtalker, practice stopping and listening; if you overdose on process, test the waters by being more decisive, beginning with less crucial issues. The key is to understand your own strengths and areas for improvement so that you can work on them, including inviting feedback from individuals and the group. It takes judgment to sort out the various cues that are coming your way—judgment that can be sharpened through practice. As Kaiser and Kaplan warn, an apparent virtue (e.g. seeking consensus) can become a vice (e.g. dithering). Judgment through reflective practice is about sorting out effective and ineffective practices.

, , ,

Kirtman's seven competencies as a group contain checks and balances; they can guide you in deciding when to be forceful and when to take more time to figure things out with others. As we have looked at the role of change agent in this chapter, I have also linked passion with skill. I've said that the marks of a change agent are relentless commitment to a cause and flexibility in how to serve that cause. To combine the two, you need to become simultaneously assertive and sensitive, demanding and understanding, confident while doubting, local and big-picture, essential at the beginning and dispensable at the end. You will need to resonate with the group all the while.

Through a discussion of Kirtman's work, I have identified a set of change-agent competencies that you will need to develop and hone. They are identifiable and learnable. They will require merging skill and passion in a way that enhances both. They will involve balancing and integrating your assertiveness and others' initiative. There has been no time in the history of the principalship that this has been more necessary than in the present. The future is now, and it is as ambiguous as it is exciting. I hope that the ideas in these first five chapters have helped you rethink the principalship and have put you in a position to proceed more confidently—as Pfeffer and Sutton put it, act with knowledge while doubting what you know.

# Action Items

☐ Take Kirtman's self-assessment inventory contained in his book. What competencies most need your attention?

☐ What are your passions? What are your strongest skills? How closely do these two lists match up?

☐ Get feedback from staff on your balance between talker and listener.

☐ Which of your strengths might you need to fear?

# Discuss with Colleagues

- Supportively describe each other as talkers and listeners.

- Apart from what districts might require, how should principals and teachers measure, keep track of, and share instructional improvement within a school?

- How should a principal move forward (and help teachers move forward) under difficult circumstances and with less than complete information?

- Do you have any what you consider "strengths" that might actually be problematic?

# CHAPTER · SIX

# The Future Is Now

I am going to be more speculative in this final chapter because the future is upon us. I don't know what will happen any more than the next person, but I do want to explore what I see in this immediate reality. Whether I am right in detail or not, no matter what happens, as principal you will need all the skills of the three roles of change that I have developed in this book.

I don't think there has ever been a time when the circumstances for the role of the principal have been more volatile. Facing the unpredictable, principals must be able to handle a good deal of ambiguity while displaying strong lead learner qualities. As one of the Irish sayings goes, "anyone who isn't confused here doesn't really understand what is going on" (cited in Gladwell, 2013, p. 222). Our change agent principals operate very well under these conditions because they help the group work toward clarity and effectiveness under difficult circumstances.

This chapter looks at two phenomena that, in my opinion, illustrate and embody formerly unforeseen forces that principals must face. One I am going to refer to as the "unplanned digital revolution," in which we are still at an early stage, the other is the relatively "planned" but also revolutionary rise of Common Core State Standards. The two can be connected, but we can initially regard and treat them independently.

## The Unplanned Digital Revolution

Of course I don't mean that no one is doing any planning relative to technological matters, but the phenomenon is so volatile that it cannot be controlled in any traditional sense of the word.

My book *Stratosphere* (2013b) raised the topic of the revolutionary potential of two dynamics working in concert. One is the
"push factor"—the fact that schooling is increasingly boring for
students and alienating for teachers (the latter caused by wider
policy conditions as well). The push factor is psychologically,
as well as literally in many cases, driving students and teachers
away from schools. The other, the "pull factor," consists of the
ever-alluring digital world. These two dynamics in interaction
pretty much guarantee that the status quo will not continue.

In *Stratosphere*, I suggested that any solution to the unstable
push-pull problem will have to meet four criteria:

---

1. Irresistibly engaging for students and teachers
2. Elegantly efficient and easy (from a technical standpoint)
   to use
3. Technologically ubiquitous 24/7
4. Steeped in real-life problem solving

---

For these criteria to be met, there will need to be a new pedagogy by which students and teachers become learning partners
(between and among each other), with students more in charge of
their own learning, and teachers as agents of change. Technology
would be an accelerator and deepener of learning in the skills
required for living and learning (which in *Stratosphere* I characterized as the six Cs: critical thinking, communication, collaboration, creativity, character, and citizenship). Predicting that
2013 would be a year of explosion of learning, I said in an effort
at flare, welcome to the stratosphere, "where you get twice the
learning for half the price." I wasn't being literal, but I do see great

potential for the role of technology in relation to costs, new learning, and new forms of leadership (Fullan & Langworthy, 2014).
Given recent rapid developments in some of the schools we are
filming, I now think that I underestimated the power of dynamic,
unplanned learning possibilities that none of us can orchestrate
(but that we can learn to participate in for our benefit).

I am going to have to be somewhat speculative, not because
none of this is happening (it is), but because we are at the early
phase of a spectacular learning revolution. By "explosion of
learning," I meant to convey that there would be thousands
of digitally based innovations occurring in multiplicative ways.
What I am seeing at this early stage is that there is explosive
action, but action accompanied by naturally occurring *patterns*.
I think that we are in the midst of a phenomenon that is positively contagious because it follows the principles of organic
change that are natural to the human condition, namely, engaging in intrinsically meaningful work, and doing it with others.

I mentioned in Chapter Four of this book that we recently
completed filming in three schools in Ontario (Fullan, 2014).
We had selected the schools as being fairly typical of those that
were integrating technology (in keeping with the four criteria
listed earlier). The schools—Park Manor and William G. Davis
Sr. (both middle schools), and Central Peel Secondary School—
have only been at this new work for three years or less. You
would have found no "plan" at the outset for what they were
about to do. There was no strong connection between the district and the schools as to what and how they would proceed.

(Incidentally, although we are not focusing on the district,
what I am describing offers important new lessons for districts.
It may not be the elaborate plan that directs effective change

but rather the encouraging of action and the reining in of what is being learned. Peel district for example, instead of carefully designing a central strategy (as was its wont in the past), signaled a change in district culture by passing a policy that embraced BYOD [Bring Your Own Device] and encouraged a culture of "yes." District leaders surmised that it would be more effective to work with the system to process what would be unleashed rather than to try to get people to behave in ways that the center determined. For unplanned change, such as the digital revolution, I believe that Peel is correct. As I will be discussing, the control is introduced as implementation unfolds—and much of that control comes from those inside the process at the school and at the district level.)

What we found in the three schools was that virtually every classroom in all three schools was abuzz with learning. We can't say that it was all exemplary, but you could see that teachers and students were excited, that technology permeated the classrooms and the school, deep learning goals were in effect, and everyone we talked to in all three schools compared the present to three years ago in terms of a change from night to day. One teacher leader who was in what she called her second career said that she had dreaded coming to school three years ago (and was contemplating a third career), and now couldn't wait to start every day. The students said that their learning environments had changed dramatically for the better. At Central Peel Secondary School, with just under a thousand students, we observed the Cross-Curricular Technology Committee, which was meeting every two weeks to share new ideas and review what was working. What used to be called the Computer Committee (before the new changes, and with six or seven teachers attending) was, on the day of our visit, bursting with some thirty teachers.

The principal of W. G. Davis said that he had known all along that the students were bored, but had not discovered that teachers had been largely unconsciously bored as well until he saw them beginning to experience a difference. We don't yet have enough hard measures of achievement, but in Park Manor, as I have already mentioned, reading and writing proficiency gauged by a very high standard had risen dramatically in the three years since the changes were introduced. In a second school, student suspension and disruption had dramatically improved. Central Peel Secondary School expected that its graduation rate, one of the lowest in the district over the past years, would immediately and steadily increase.

That these changes happened so quickly and without much planning caught me off guard. But when you consider them from the perspective of natural change processes, they make sense. You start with a bad situation—stodgy schooling; school leaders begin to look outside (as described in Chapter Five) to see what is happening; they engage staff and students in building a vision; they embrace a BYOD philosophy; they start trying new things with the attitude of willingness to see what works; they establish parameters for what is acceptable and to be retained or not; and they measure their success by engagement and learning outcomes.

It is working so well because it has the qualities of a social epidemic or positive contagion. People take to change when it is intrinsically interesting and when they have some say in its evolution, develop ownership with others, and enjoy doing something worthwhile with peers inside and outside their schools.

The process might appear to be leaderless, but when you examine it closely, it has all the markings of being based on the professional capital model. Organic change, naturally occurring change, is by definition not tightly planned and controlled, but if you ask the question, "Where is the glue that enables such a system to find coherence?" you readily find it in the kind of leadership discussed throughout this book. I identified at least seven main elements of success that prevailed in these schools:

1. **Vision and goals**. Leaders worked hard with others to create and fashion a jointly owned, clear framework; in Park Manor it was the Accelerated Learning Framework, and in the high school it was the Central Peel 21st Century Learning Framework—in both cases displayed and referred to in every classroom.

2. **Resources**. Principals and the district worked to enable the schools to be broadband wireless, to acquire technology, and to establish job-embedded time to work together.

3. **Exemplary pedagogy**. People were identifying and sharing what works in the new learning partnership between and among students and teachers.

4. **Data**. Learning is more personalized to the student, with diagnosis of progress linked explicitly to actions to improve learning.

5. **Digital citizenship**. BYOD policies are broadly permissive but are mediated by specific norms and rules that have been jointly worked out with students. W. G. Davis, for example, has a Digital Citizenship forum for all students for an hour every second week (which frees up teachers for planning). In the digital world, changes are occurring so

quickly that you have to work constantly to remain on top of how technology is being used.

6. **Proliferation of leadership**. School principals develop other leaders who in turn develop still others—teachers and students alike.

7. **Unbounded learning**. Principals free staff from boundaries and encourage and enable teachers and classes to access people and ideas within the school and district, and worldwide.

In these processes, the principal in each case is a key but not necessarily dominant player in any given breakthrough. When I asked Andreas Meyer, principal of W. G. Davis, how he perceived his role, he responded without hesitation that it was "to get out of the way." He knew this was an exaggeration, but it had a basic truth to it. He had played a strong initial role at the beginning (three years before) in getting things started, focusing on human capital and helping get things under way, but once the school was in full flight, he saw his role as one of keeping engaged as much as a participant as a formal leader. As he put it, now that teachers are so engaged, he needs to take two steps back so that teachers can take three steps forward.

The high school principal, Lawrence De Maeyer, described his role as "under construction," but then he had no trouble describing its evolution. He said, "At first I thought it was my job to advocate good ideas and get them around, but now I see that I need to enable people to share what they are doing, and give them a platform to do this—to share works in progress. He elaborated, "I need to provide structures for sharing, be less prescriptive, listen more, talk less, and support innovators by finding ways to make new things happen. I spend a lot of time talking to students and teachers as they tell me what they are doing, and I can cross-link it to other examples in the school." He then said that now that new things are under way, they have shifted the conversation to how they are going to measure how well the students are doing. He concluded by saying, "I have learned an enormous amount from staff and students." With all this technology around, he said, "My job is to help people connect it to learning."

There is another change lesson in all of this; my colleague Rick DuFour pointed it out when he read a draft of this book. In the past, we had both been attracted to Teresa Amabile and Steven Kramer's research (2011) on what they refer to as the "progress principle." (On the business administration faculty at Harvard, Amabile studies how everyday life inside organizations can influence people and their performance, an interest shared by Kramer, a research psychologist.) They found that people are most motivated, energized, and self-efficacious when they feel that they have overcome obstacles and made progress, even small steps of progress in their daily work. They also found that the negative effects of butting into obstacles or otherwise not getting anywhere carry three times more negative weight than making progress carries positive weight. Thus, frequent small positive steps are three times more valuable than being stuck. I think that the progress principle is in effect at the three schools. The principals, encouraged by their districts, are creating the conditions that help people succeed. This means removing obstacles, providing resources, and supporting autonomy and group development, and then calling attention to the progress though celebration. This works because it is in keeping with the natural desires of the human spirit, namely, to do something intrinsically worthwhile with others in a collective effort. There is a big lesson in change here for the future of the principalship, and indeed for all leadership.

I am not suggesting a panacea, but mainly trying to loosen up our thinking and action. Change under these circumstances may be more natural and organic than we have hitherto thought. You can see, for example, how my "twice the learning for half the price" passing remark might easily become a reality (or at least twice the learning for the same price)—if students became the technology experts for teachers; if students helped teach other students; if the learning day was doubled as students conducted purposeful work outside of school hours as they also became more engaged in learning during the day. All of this has very important implications for leaders at the school, district, and state levels.

The trends that I have just featured will, indeed, take off on a large scale. I have no doubt that many more schools among Peel's 246 will quickly jump on the opportunity—as will other schools and systems that follow this general path. We will move from a few boutique schools featuring phenomenal technology to a widespread normality of these new ways of learning.

What these developments tell us about leadership is quite revealing. Under these more dynamic conditions leadership might be a matter of stimulating then cultivating naturally occurring phenomena, when the opportunity presents itself. My colleagues and I continue to develop the ideas from *Stratosphere*. For one project, we developed an index for assessing digital innovations according to the three components of technology, pedagogy, and system potential (Fullan & Donnelly, 2013). For another, we are establishing a large network of schools around the world to develop and share the kinds of ideas that we have already seen in the schools we filmed (Fullan & Langworthy, 2013, 2014). I predict that these naturally occurring examples will spread and proliferate like contagion because of the push-pull dynamic that exists in so many classrooms.

# Planned Change: Common Core State Standards

It may seem like going from the sublime to the ridiculous, but if you are a principal in the United States, you have to be preoccupied with the CCSS. Ever since No Child Left Behind began in 2002, states have been required to have standards for literacy, numeracy, and the like. But for several years there were no particular guidelines for determining which standards to develop—no standards for the standards, so to speak. Consequently, the actual standards sprang up literally and figuratively all over the map. To make a recent long story short, in 2010, state leaders from forty-six states published CCSS in English language arts (ELA, including history, social studies, science, and technical studies) and in mathematics. Moreover, they established two large multistate consortia (one called Partnership for Assessment of Readiness for College and Careers PARCC the other named Smarter Balanced Assessment Consortia), with the federal government funding them to the tune of almost half a billion dollars to develop "assessment instruments aligned to the standards." For a primer on CCSS, see Kendall, 2011; John Kendall is a senior director of research at the Mid-Continent Research for Education and Learning lab. A more detailed political history of the development of CCSS has been written by Robert Rothman (2011), an expert in assessment and now a senior fellow at the Alliance for Excellent Education.

The standards themselves are demanding—world class, as they say (for a complete list of the standards, see www .corestandards.org/the-standards). For example, in both ELA and math, students are to construct, write responses to, and evaluate arguments. Schools can no longer be a place where information is merely presented; students must be actively engaged in their own learning—building deep understanding of concepts, applying different frameworks, analyzing the work of others, finding solutions to real problems through collaboration, thinking creatively and critically, contributing ideas, and developing products of quality. Among other things, the CCSS standards in ELA call for students to read and comprehend texts of progressively increasing "text complexity." All of this entails a significant change in the learning roles of the teacher and the student (and among teachers and students) on a massive scale. Thus we see that CCSS contains all the dilemmas, traps, and opportunities for the principal that we have been discussing in previous chapters.

Think of a stool, the legs of which are standards, assessment, and learning (the latter referring to instruction, pedagogy, and curriculum). The original CCSS framework stated that it would leave the third domain—instruction—to teachers, although New York State, for example, has begun to specify the instruction for ELA. No matter who is responsible for it, this third leg represents an enormously deep and difficult change. My point is that nobody really knows how to integrate standards, assessment, and instruction on a large scale, and those who think they have the answer could never pull it off at the implementation stage. As for the role of technology in CCSS, it seems more linked to accessing online assessment of student learning than to how to improve instruction.

Because the third leg of the stool—instruction and learning—is still undefined in CCSS, we are back to the principal and the ideas of professional capital that this book has been about. We are not talking about leading the implementation of a previously proven practice. With CCSS we are instead dealing with leadership for *innovations* in a domain where no one knows in advance what is likely to work. I must say that if we take the perspective of a planner—someone in charge of implementing CCSS systemwide—I don't like the chances. From that perch, the innovations look likely to come out much too top-heavy and complex to work on any scale. One can predict that many states will drop out the closer they get to implementation. We are already seeing this phenomenon as several states have left the PARCC group.

Something like CCSS is needed because current standards in the United States are so low. But instead of taking the passive position that it is your job to implement the CCSS, take the proactive stance of looking at what is in CCSS that you find valuable and that can help lead implementation. Use the three leadership roles in this book to implement high-level standards that will benefit the students you serve. Don't stake your future on CCSS per se, but rather on the deep learning goals that standards ideally represent. Don't be thrown if CCSS per se wanes; even if it does, your underlying goals will still relate to the deep learning goals that are being espoused these days (the six Cs I noted earlier) and to a new pedagogical partnership between students and teachers, which Maria Langworthy and I describe in follow-up work from *Stratosphere* (Fullan & Langworthy, 2014).

My message is that as a school leader, you should understand the big picture but also work from the ground up. If you can help your school identify a core agenda while you help local members also plug into the bigger picture, you will always do more good than you would trying to figure out what the system wants. Developing the professional capital of your teachers will always put you in good stead for deciding what to do under conditions of uncertainty.

## Time to Change Careers? Or to Change Gears?

Do you still want the job? Seriously, you know that the job is exciting—a moral imperative platform the likes of which has never before been seen by school leaders. It is your opportunity to develop skills to a level that you become "so good they can't ignore you." In their book *Great by Choice* (2011), Jim Collins ("student and teacher of enduring great companies") and Morten Hansen (management professor at UC Berkeley) wrote about leaders who were especially successful under difficult circumstances (in other words, under conditions that are becoming all too normal). They found that such leaders contend well with uncertainty and chaos, and deal well with "luck," bad or otherwise. Specifically, they characterize these leaders as having three traits: fanatic discipline (think of focused, persistent innovation in CCSS and technology); empirical creativity (they learn from good data; they change their minds when it is called for); and productive paranoia (they're always aware that they might be missing something). These three qualities should ring true to you.

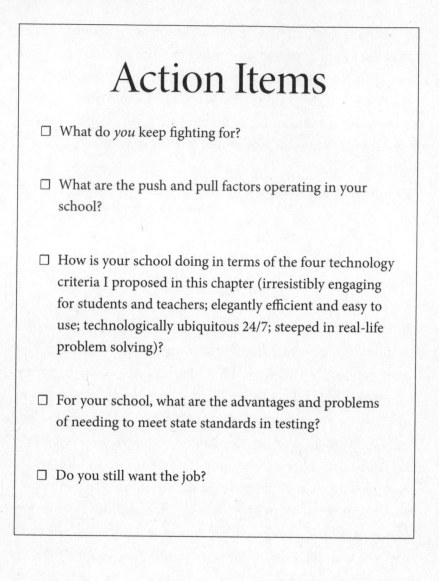

# Action Items

☐ What do *you* keep fighting for?

☐ What are the push and pull factors operating in your school?

☐ How is your school doing in terms of the four technology criteria I proposed in this chapter (irresistibly engaging for students and teachers; elegantly efficient and easy to use; technologically ubiquitous 24/7; steeped in real-life problem solving)?

☐ For your school, what are the advantages and problems of needing to meet state standards in testing?

☐ Do you still want the job?

# Discuss with Colleagues

- If you are in a state that has adopted CCSS, what are their pros and cons as you consider the next two or three years?

- What is digital technology accomplishing right now in your schools? What potential haven't you tapped?

- What will it take for your school and district to become "so good they can't ignore you"?

- Where is your school or district now in terms of Collins and Hansen's fanatic discipline, empirical creativity, and productive paranoia?

# A Final Word

Twenty-five years ago, I ended *What's Worth Fighting for in the Principalship* with this marvelous passage from George Bernard Shaw's *Man and Superman*. It seems apropos to take up the torch once more:

This is the true joy in life, the being used for a purpose recognized by yourself as a mighty one; the being a force of nature instead of a feverish, selfish little clod of ailments and grievances complaining that the world will not devote itself to making you happy. I am of the opinion that my life belongs to the whole community, and as long as I live it is my privilege to do for it whatever I can. I want to be thoroughly used up when I die, for the harder I work the more I live. I rejoice in life for its own sake. Life is no "brief candle" to me. It is a sort of splendid torch which I have got hold of for the moment, and I want to make it burn as brightly as possible before handing it on to future generations.

Under current conditions, when the system does not necessarily know what it is doing, principals have enormous responsibilities. If you are proactive, you will find the role deeply fulfilling, and you will be appreciated on many fronts. The principalship today—a critical role meets a vibrant opportunity. So, principals, you are needed more than ever—maximize your impact while you have the chance!

# REFERENCES

Australian Institute for Teaching and School Leadership. (2012). *Australian teacher performance and development framework*. Melbourne: Author.

Amabile, T., & Kramer, S. (2011). *The progress principle: Using small wins to ignite joy, engagement, and creativity at work*. Boston, MA: Harvard Business Review Press.

Anderson, J. (2013, March 30). Curious grade for teachers: Nearly all pass. *New York Times*. http://www.nytimes.com/2013/03/31/education/curious-grade-for-teachers-nearly-all-pass.html?pagewanted=all&_r=0.

Brion, S., & Anderson, C. (2013). The loss of power: How illusions of alliance contribute to powerholders' downfall. *Organizational Behavior and Human Decision Processes, 121,* 129–139.

Bryk, A., Bender-Sebring, P., Allensworth, E., Lupescu, S., & Easton, J. (2010). *Organizing schools for improvement: Lessons from Chicago*. Chicago, IL: University of Chicago Press.

Bryk, A., & Schneider, B. (2002). *Trust in schools*. New York, NY: Russell Sage.

California Office to Reform Education. (2012). *CORE: Mission and Goals.* Sacramento, CA: Author.

California Office to Reform Education. (2013). School Quality Improvement System. http://coredistricts.org/school-quality-improvement-system/

City, E. A., Elmore, R. F., Fiarman, S. E., & Teitel, L. (2009). *Instructional rounds in education.* Cambridge, MA: Harvard Education Press.

Cole, P. (2004). Professional development: A great way to avoid change. Seminar Series 194. Melbourne: Centre for Strategic Education.

Cole, P. (2013). Aligning professional learning, performance management and effective teaching. Seminar Series 217. Melbourne: Centre for Strategic Education.

Collins, J., & Hansen, M. (2011). *Great by choice.* New York, NY: HarperBusiness.

Corcoran, A., Casserly, M., Price-Baugh, R., Walston, D., Hall, R., & Simon, C. (2013). *Rethinking leadership: The changing role of principal supervisors.* New York: The Wallace Foundation.

Covey, S. (2004). *The 7 habits of highly effective people.* New York, NY: Simon & Schuster.

Cuban, L. (2013). *Inside the black box of classroom practice.* Cambridge, MA: Harvard Education Press.

David, J., & Talbert, J. (2013). *Turning around a high poverty district.* San Francisco, CA: S. H. Cowell Foundation.

DuFour, R., & Fullan, M. (2013). *Built to last: Systemic PLCs at work*. Bloomington, IN: Solution Tree.

DuFour, R., & Marzano, R. (2009). High-leverage strategies for principal leadership. *Educational Leadership*, 66(5), 62–68.

DuFour, R., & Mattos, M. (2013). How do principals really improve schools? *Educational Leadership*, 70(7), 34–40.

Edmonton Public Schools, District No. 7. (2013). *Community of practice in Edmonton Public Schools*. Alberta: Author.

Emotional breakdown. (2013, April 6). *Economist*, p. 78.

Fullan, M. (1988). *What's worth fighting for in the principalship*. Toronto: Ontario Public School Teachers' Federation.

Fullan, M. (2010a). *All systems go*. Thousand Oaks, CA: Corwin Press.

Fullan, M. (2010b). *Motion leadership: The skinny on becoming change savvy*. Thousand Oaks: CA: Corwin Press.

Fullan, M. (2011a). Choosing the wrong drivers for whole system reform. Seminar Series 204. Melbourne: Centre for Strategic Education.

Fullan, M. (2011b). *Change leader: Learning to do what matters most*. San Francisco, CA: Jossey-Bass.

Fullan, M. (2011c). *Moral imperative realized*. Thousand Oaks, CA: Corwin Press.

Fullan, M. (2013a). *Motion leadership in action*. Thousand Oaks, CA: Corwin Press.

Fullan, M. (2013b). *Stratosphere: Integrating technology, pedagogy and change knowledge.* Toronto: Pearson.

Fullan, M. (2014). Motion Leadership Film Series. www .michaelfullan.ca

Fullan, M., & Donnelly, K. (2013). *Alive in the swamp: Assessing digital innovations in education.* London: NESTA; New York, NY: New Schools Venture Fund.

Fullan, M., & Langworthy, M. (2013). *Towards a new end: New pedagogies for deep learning.* Seattle, WA: Collaborative Impact.

Fullan, M., & Langworthy, M. (2014). *A rich seam: How new pedagogies find deep learning.* Report commissioned by the office of Sir Michael Barber, chief education adviser to Pearson. London: Pearson.

Gladwell, M. (2008). *Outliers: The story of success.* New York, NY: Little, Brown.

Gladwell, M. (2013). *David and Goliath: Underdogs, misfits, and the art of battling giants.* New York: Little, Brown.

Hargreaves, A., & Braun, H. (2012). *Leading for all.* Final report to the Council of Directors of Education. Boston, MA: Boston College.

Hargreaves, A., & Fullan, M. (2012). *Professional capital: Transforming teaching in every school.* New York, NY: Teachers College Press.

Hattie, J. (2009). *Visible learning: A synthesis of over 800 meta-analyses relating to achievement.* London: Routledge.

Hattie, J. (2012). *Visible learning for teachers.* New York, NY: Routledge.

Honig, M., Copland, M., Rainey, L., Lorton, J., & Newton, M. (2010, April). *Central office transformation for district-wide teaching and learning improvement.* Seattle, WA: Center for the Study of Teaching and Policy.

Jenkins, L. (2013). *Permission to forget.* Milwaukee, WI: American Society for Quality Press.

Johnson, S. (2010). *Where good ideas come from.* New York: Riverhead Books.

Kaplan, R., & Kaiser, R. (2013). *Fear your strengths: What you are best at could be your biggest problem.* New York, NY: Basic Books.

Kendall, J. (2011). *Understanding Common Core State Standards.* Alexandria, VA: Association for Supervision and Curriculum Development.

Kirp, D. L. (2013). *Improbable scholars.* New York, NY: Oxford University Press.

Kirtman, L. (2013). *Leadership and teams: The missing piece of the education reform puzzle.* Upper Saddle River, NJ: Pearson Education.

Kotter, J. (2008). *A sense of urgency.* Boston, MA: Harvard Business Press.

Leana, C. R. (2011). The missing link in school reform. *Stanford Social Innovation Review, 9*(4), 30–35.

Leithwood, K. (2011). *Characteristics of high performing school districts in Ontario.* Toronto: OISE/University of Toronto.

Leithwood, K., & Seashore Louis, K. (2012). *Linking leadership to student learning.* San Francisco, CA: Jossey-Bass.

Leithwood, K., Seashore Louis, K., Anderson, S., & Wahlstrom, K. (2004). *How leadership influences student learning*. New York, NY: Wallace Foundation.

Liker, J., & Meier, D. (2007). *Toyota talent*. New York, NY: McGraw-Hill.

Mehta, J. (2013). *The allure of order: High hopes, dashed expectations, and the troubled quest to remake American schooling*. New York, NY: Oxford University Press.

Metropolitan Life Insurance Company. (2013). *The MetLife survey of the American teacher*. New York, NY: Author.

National Commission on Excellence in Education. (1983). *A nation at risk*. Washington, DC: U.S. Government Printing Office.

New Jersey Department of Education. (2013). *Student growth objectives: Developing and using practical measures of student learning*. Trenton, NJ: Author.

Newport, C. (2012). *So good they can't ignore you: Why skills trump passion in the quest for work you love*. New York, NY: Business Plus.

Office for Standards in Education. (2013). *Unseen children: Access and achievement 20 years on*. London: Author.

Organisation for Economic Co-operation and Development. (2013). *Teachers for the 21st century: Using evaluation to improve teaching*. Paris: Author.

Pfeffer, J., & Sutton, R. I. (2006). *Hard facts, dangerous half-truths, and total nonsense*. Boston, MA: Harvard Business School Press.

Pink, D. (2009). *Drive: The surprising truth about what motivates us.* New York, NY: Riverhead Books.

Robinson, K. (2013). *Finding your element.* New York, NY: Viking.

Robinson, V. (2011). *Student-centered leadership.* San Francisco, CA: Jossey-Bass.

Robinson, V., Lloyd, C., & Rowe, K. (2008). The impact of leadership on student outcomes. *Education Administration Quarterly, 44,* 635–674.

Rothman, R. (2011). *Something in common: The next chapter in American education.* Boston, MA: Harvard Education Publishing Group.

Teitel, L. (2013). *School-based instructional rounds.* Cambridge, MA. Harvard Education Press.

Timperley, H. (2011). *Realizing the power of professional learning.* New York, MA: McGraw-Hill.

Tucker, M. (2013). True or false: Teacher evaluations improve accountability, raise achievement. Top Performers (*Education Week* blog), July 18, 2013, http://blogs.edweek.org/edweek/top_performers/2013/07/true_or_false_teacher_evaluations_improve_accountability_raise_achievement.html.

Turnbull, B., Riley, D., Arcaira, E., Anderson, L. & MacFarlane, J. (2013). *Six districts begin the pipeline initiative.* New York, NY: Wallace Foundation.

Wells, C. M., & Feun, L. (2013). Education change and professional learning communities: A study of two districts. *Journal of Educational Change, 14,* 233–257.

# INDEX